Paranormal Investigations

Paranormal Investigations

THE PROPER PROCEDURES AND PROTOCOLS OF
INVESTIGATION FOR THE BEGINNER TO THE PRO

Chad Stambaugh

iUNIVERSE, INC.
BLOOMINGTON

PARANORMAL INVESTIGATIONS
THE PROPER PROCEDURES AND PROTOCOLS OF INVESTIGATION FOR THE BEGINNER TO THE PRO

iUniverse books may be ordered through booksellers or by contacting:

iUniverse
1663 Liberty Drive
Bloomington, IN 47403
www.iuniverse.com
1-800-Authors (1-800-288-4677)

ISBN: 978-1-4759-7163-7 (sc)
ISBN: 978-1-4759-7164-4 (hc)
ISBN: 978-1-4759-7165-1 (e)

Library of Congress Control Number: 2013900782

Printed in the United States of America

iUniverse rev. date: 1/14/2013

To my wife, Crissy; my kids, Chrystal, Vinnie, and Ana; and my grandchildren, Haylie and Gavin.

Table of Contents

Preface

The first and most important thing that I want to stress from the beginning is that the methods and procedures that I talk about are my opinion. They're not the only ways of doing an investigation. However, most of the reputable people in the paranormal field that I have investigated with or have talked to extensively, use the very methods that I will talk to you about here in my book. I've taken the best ideas and methods and put them together in what I believe to be a concise and proper way an investigation should be handled. And I'm not talking about the high-profile celebrities on TV who, in my opinion, have lost their way due to the stardom that their shows have given them. If you watch these shows, you'll notice all kinds of different ways to perform an investigation. Some are good, some are very wrong and dangerous, and some are even just downright ridiculous. Nor am I talking about the charlatans who parade themselves at Para conferences. No, I'm talking about the ones who do this on a daily basis, day in and day out—not those who do it just one day a week or during a weekend and say "look at me" and want to get paid for it. I am referring to those people who are out there on a daily basis to actually help people who have problems with their homes or businesses—those people who need and want to understand what is going on so that they can deal with it or, in some cases, want whatever it is gone so they can have their lives back. These very dedicated and professional few are who I base my methods and procedures on.

I think that those of us in the paranormal field will finally be taken seriously by not only the mainstream but also by the scientific arena if every single person or team of investigators uses these simple yet effective methods in every single investigation they perform. Whether you are on the East Coast or West Coast of the United States, in Europe, Africa, South America, or anywhere in between, everyone needs to use the same methods and procedures. Once this is accomplished, we will no longer be looked at as a bunch of crazy crackpots who are just running around like little kids in a candy store, seeing ghosts at every turn and proclaiming that we know what we're doing. Because of a lack of consistency in our current methods, we cannot prove anything because we are not taken seriously.

As for equipment, not one piece of equipment, unfortunately, has been invented to unequivocally and scientifically prove the existence of spirits. I will, however, show you some methods and ideas that, I feel, will make it arguably easier to possibly prove that ghosts do exist and harder for the scientific skeptics to prove us wrong. However, the equipment that we do have at our disposal is pretty good at getting some, let's say, "interesting" conclusions, if used properly and uniformly everywhere. I will not say that they prove unequivocally that ghosts exist. What I will say, though, is that they can produce some interesting conclusions that need to be looked at closer because of the unexplained results that they sometimes create.

This book, *Paranormal Investigations*, will also hopefully create a feeling of something else that this field desperately needs to be taken seriously in the mainstream. That feeling is *paranormal unity*. If every team or individual uses the same methods and learns to work together as a larger forum and gets rid of what I like to call the ego factor, we can, as a field, come together and get some real work done to finally prove that ghosts exist! Until this happens, we can't get rid of the Para-drama that is too prevalent in our field. The paranormal field is not a competition; it supposed to be about cooperation. Okay, enough of my personal opinions; let's get started with what this book is all about.

The procedures and methods that will be explained here will be split into two groups. The first will be for people with an interest in investigating historical sites, sites used for paranormal conventions (or Para cons) that you're visiting, or just fun places to investigate.

The people who like to perform these kinds of investigations are what I call ghost hunters. Why? Because all ghost hunters want to do is go on the investigation. They will check their evidence that night but won't check all of it, or they won't check it at all. I know some investigators who have evidence from years before and still haven't reviewed their evidence. Now before you jump all over me and say, "Maybe that's all I want to do!" well, that's great, and I have no problem with it. Those types of investigations have their place. Heck, I even do them!

What I have a problem with is when people investigate a private residence and all they do is give the client their evidence. Maybe they say to the client, "Yes, we think that something might be happening here." What if the client wants the spirit gone? Or even an explanation as to why the spirit is there? Maybe the client wants to know how to handle it or how to take his or her house back. A ghost hunter will just say, "Sorry, but we don't do that," and leave the client hanging. A paranormal investigator not only does the investigation but also will help the client get rid of the spirit/entity (if possible), council his or her client as to why the spirit was there, and help the client understand what is possibly going on. They will also help educate clients on how to empower themselves so that they can protect themselves and take back control of their lives. That's the difference between the two. So, in my opinion, if the ghost hunter is not willing to take the next step and get the education to help the client completely, he or she should not delve into private, client-based investigations. This does more harm than good.

Now, if the ghost hunter wants to move on to the next phase, this can be achieved once he or she has advanced beyond what we call weekend warrior syndrome (I'm stealing this phrase from my military days). You're now ready to take this more seriously and help people who need our help. You're getting the education that you need to help clients by seeking out other experienced investigators or teams that are willing to teach this aspect of the business. You're reading books, taking classes: these resources are out there; you just have to look for them. At the end of this book is a list of reputable teams and organizations out there that do just that. I encourage you to reach out to these awesome teams. They will gladly help you out.

Some of the procedures that I will show you can be used in both fun and client-based investigations. The main reason I say they're different and that you need different procedures and protocols in handling a private investigation than you do a fun investigation (which again is what I consider an investigation of a historical site or a Para con) is that the private investigations have legal ramifications. So because there are a few more procedures that need to be followed with a private investigation, I need to break the two up for you to get the correct feel for how they each should be handled.

Acknowledgments

I didn't get to where I'm at and obtain the knowledge that I have today without some great people and organizations. Therefore, I want to give appreciation to those who have given me their time, energy, and unending patience to show me how to do this job the right way. I give gratitude to United Paranormal International and the people who run it for believing in me and my experience as a paranormal investigator and then putting me in a position to help them make their organization better. Another one that I'd like to acknowledge is the Lightworkers Foundation of Fresno, who gave my wife, Crissy, and I some great avenues to flourish in our work.

I'd like to give thanks to the following people who helped guide me with a better understanding of the paranormal: Thomas Durant, Benny and Heather Huerta, Peggy Armer, and Jackie Meador. Without these people, I would still be a lost puppy in the woods.

Introduction

For the beginner—someone just getting into what the paranormal is all about—let me explain some things before getting into the meat and potatoes. The paranormal is a rather broad field and has come to generally include all types of mysterious phenomena. The word "paranormal" basically means "above the normal." It can apply to just about anything we do not yet understand and that has not yet been scientifically proven. The most common aspects of the paranormal field include different categories, such as ghosts, parapsychology (which studies psychological phenomena), UFOs, and cryptozoology (which studies unknown animals). All of these categories are considered to be the study of metaphysics. This is the study of the existence and consciousness of the unknown. The study of paranormal and anomalous phenomena is a must to gain more insight into the human condition, both now and when we die. The study of metaphysics will enhance your knowledge of the paranormal from what you've seen or heard on TV.

You're probably asking why someone would get into this field or even believe in it. I don't follow organized religion per se, but I am a spiritual person. I've always wondered about the other side and where we go when we leave this existence. So delving into the paranormal for me was a natural progression from just wondering to actually performing investigations. I'm going to share a couple of my personal experiences that prove to me that there are spirits.

One day, while at home with my daughter, I witnessed a one-cup measuring scoop fly across the room and hit my daughter in the head.

No one was in the kitchen but my daughter, who was a good six feet away from the scoop, which we use to feed the animals. This house is my wife's house, and her grandmother had died in it some years back. Before I ever moved in, she had experiences with her grandmother, who originally owned the house. All of the animals were accounted for, and just five minutes before this I had asked my daughter to feed the animals, and she had not done it yet. To me, this was grandma's way of reminding my daughter to feed the animals.

Another time, I was feeding my grandson in his high chair, and we were the only humans in the house at the time. Not even any of the animals were in the house—I checked. We have all our furniture—a sofa, a love seat, and a recliner that my wife sits in—against one side of the house. The recliner is situated in between the couch and love seat. The recliner faces directly at the other wall, where the TV is located. And this recliner is pretty heavy; you have to actually sit in it to move it. Well, I was feeding my grandson in his high chair while sitting on the sofa, facing away from the recliner. A couple of moments into feeding my grandson, he started looking over my shoulder like he was watching someone behind me. I thought nothing of it at first. A few more minutes went by, and just out of curiosity, I turned around and asked my grandson, "Who are you looking at?" Then, for no real reason other than that it just popped into my head, I said, "Is there anyone else here with us today?" As soon as I said that, the recliner made a forty-five-degree turn toward me and my grandson. Needless to say, I immediately got goose bumps. So I said, "Grandma, if that's you, can you turn the chair back to its rightful position?" No sooner had I said this than it turned back to its rightful position. All I could say in my shock was "Thank you!" And so, my involvement into paranormal investigating began.

With all the different ghost hunting shows on the air and all the different ways that you have seen investigations performed on TV, have you ever wondered how to do your own paranormal investigation? I did. Where do you go to learn about doing this? Are there people out there who teach you how to do this? Quite frankly, I didn't know. So my wife and I started a search online to see if there was anything or anyone in our area that could help us with that. We found a paranormal group in our local Fresno, California, area and found out that the leader actually taught classes. So we took her six-week course and had our final exam, which was an actual investigation at a local hotel/resort that was proclaimed to be haunted.

To our surprise, and excitement, we actually got some really good evidence. When we got that first EVP, it was like I was five years old again and I was with my grandmother when she took me to the local five-and-dime store. Yes I'm showing my age here, but you know the feeling. You walk in there, and on the side of the wall is all that penny candy, and your grandma gives you a whole dollar and says, "Get whatever you want." Your eyes go wide with excitement because you just hit the jackpot! Of course she later clarifies that you have to share it with your sister and cousins who are also staying at Grandma's. But you get the point. Hearing that first captured EVP is like getting all that candy. It was a fantastic evening. From there we met some other groups and started to investigate with them. We started investigating all sorts of unique and interesting places. Two years later, we started our own team, 11th Hour Paranormal, and the rest is history.

Okay, so enough about me. This is a book after all, about how to investigate. I hope that this will help you understand, in layman's terms, how to do a proper investigation. All the books that I have read or heard about are either just stories of that author's or group's experience, or they get so technical and scientific that it goes over my head and makes no sense. I want to keep this as simple as possible for us average people. But let's talk about some other things first.

CHAPTER ONE

What Is a Ghost?

W hat are ghosts? I'll give you the answer straight out: no one knows for certain. There are, however, many theories to explain the thousands of experiences that people around the world have had. I think ghosts and spirits are a common part of the so-called human experience. There also appear to be several types of ghosts or hauntings, and more than one theory might be needed to explain them all.

The traditional view of a ghost is that it is the spirit of a dead person who for some reason is stuck between this world and the next, often as a result of some tragedy or trauma. I believe that some of these earthbound spirits don't know they are dead. Others know they are dead but remain because they are attached to someone, something, or some place. These ghosts/spirits are what I believe to be an "intelligent haunt." These ghosts exist in a kind of limbo state in which they haunt the scenes of their deaths or locations that were pleasant to them in life. I often think that these types of ghosts are able to interact with the living, and on occasion they can even materialize. As an investigator, I try to communicate with them in hopes of a response.

On the other hand, some ghosts appear to be mere recordings on the environment in which they once existed: A soldier is seen on repeated occasions staring out a window where he once stood watch. A child's laughter is heard in a hallway where the child once played. There are even cases of ghost trains that can still be heard and sometimes seen, even though the tracks they ran on are long gone. These types of ghosts do not interact with or seem to be aware of the living as much as an intelligent ghost. Their appearance and actions seem to always be the same. To me it's like a spirit-level recording, or residual energy, which replays over and over again, as if in a loop. We call these "residual" ghosts/spirits.

One of my theories concerning a residual haunt is that these entities are actually what have been called a "thought form." I think that some of the most famous ghosts are commonly referred to as residual hauntings and are suspected to be a "thought-form" ghost. These ghosts were created by some sort of emotional disturbance, such as a suicide, a war, or even a natural death, and grew through the energy of people believing in them and adding their thoughts and energy, which in turn provide an ongoing source of power for them. When such hauntings occur, is there a way to find out if the ghost is a thought form? I think one way of finding out is to do some research. While researching the location, if you find out that nothing has been documented to support the claims but the story of the ghost has been passed down through the generations, then you may have a thought-form entity. As paranormal investigators, these are conclusions that we try to reach.

Are there such things as ghosts? The phenomena of ghosts and hauntings are very real experiences that more and more people are experiencing every day. It is their true cause and nature that is the ongoing mystery. This is what keeps me and many others investigating more and more places: trying to find that one piece of evidence that will finally prove, without any doubt, that ghosts are real.

Okay, let's finally begin our education into the world of investigating. The first thing we are going to look at is what we need to actually do an investigation. The next chapter starts out with the basics, and we'll build from there.

CHAPTER TWO

Basic Tools: Pen, Paper, Flashlight, Watch, and You

Most ghost hunters think you need a lot of cool tools and gadgets to get started in the field of paranormal investigating, but that is simply not true. The most important tools to have with you on an investigation are a pen, some paper, a flashlight, a watch, and your own eyes and ears. You might be saying to yourself, "How can that be?" Well, let me break it down for you. During an investigation, you should keep a log of everything. This is where the pen, paper, and watch come in. These logs should include investigation, time, weather, any experiences that you might have, photos, EMF/temperature baselines (if you have the necessary tools), and anything else you think is relevant. A description of a few of those logs is as follows:

Investigation (timetable) is used to document things such as what time you arrived at the location, what time you started investigating, who investigated and where (and at what times), where each investigator was constantly, what equipment you used, etc. This log will help you keep track of the investigation and assist with review process.

Weather is used to document the weather conditions at the time of the investigation. We also recommend you check the moon cycles. We use this information to track weather conditions on the day of an investigation if data is captured so we can compare it to other similar events in other cases. It will also help you during the review process in case you discover lots of orbs (could be rain) or mists (could be an investigator's breath).

Experience is used to document all personal experiences (or equipment malfunctions) during an investigation. Make sure to document everything you can remember about each experience so you have the information for future reference. During an investigation, you should make safety your first priority. To assist with that, always have a flashlight on you. The use of a flashlight is important, especially on stairs or in a room you aren't familiar with. However, it is best to keep the usage to a minimum. Your eyes will adjust to the dark, and you'll be able to observe more activity with the naked eye. We use flashlights with red lenses so that our eyes aren't affected by the light. While you are investigating, use your eyes and ears to take in everything around you and be observant. Sometimes it is best to just sit quietly and observe the space around you. This will help to debunk situations that occur as well as observe any activity that may exist. This doesn't mean you have to be silent 100 percent of the time, but silence is a friend to investigators. As you are observing, make sure to never lose the skeptic in you. Whenever a potential paranormal experience occurs, try to debunk it. Check for natural causes, such as wind, rain, etc. Check to see if someone or something else was in the area at the time. Check for something in the space that could cause the noise, such as a furnace, dripping faucet, window, door, etc. Also, try to rule out the obvious before assuming its proof of paranormal activity.

As you can see, you can do a lot with those simple tools and for little money. Once you get these techniques down, then you are ready to move onto the other tools, such as a digital recorder, digital camera, EMF detector, thermometer, or video camera.

CHAPTER THREE

Equipment

B efore we can even get into the procedures and protocols regarding how a paranormal investigation should be run, we need to talk about the equipment. I don't know how many times I've gone on an investigation, whether it is a fun investigation or a private investigation, with other investigators. The most common problem I see is that a lot of people go out and buy all the great different pieces of equipment that can be used in an investigation, but they don't know how to properly use them. If you're going to use a piece of equipment, you need to know not only what it's used for, but also the proper way of using it. I don't blame anyone for not using a piece of equipment properly unless he or she is part of a team. The fact is that some of the directions you get with these pieces of equipment are so technical that unless you're a tech genius, you have no idea what they mean.

Also, because some of these pieces of equipment actually have other purposes for which they were invented, they don't even have directions on how to use them in a paranormal setting. So an individual might not know or have access to knowledge on how to use a certain piece of equipment properly. Unfortunately, that's also the problem with some teams—no one on the team knows how to use the equipment properly, so the whole team ends up not properly trained. Thus, this results in there being a lot of people in the field who don't know how to use their equipment properly.

I haven't been to a lot of Para conferences, because I don't feel like paying for all the hype. The ones I've been to, though, have been great. No big celebrity names; just real, down-home investigators that want to share their knowledge. I've been to enough conferences to notice one thing: the one thing I've never seen taught at a conference is how to properly use the equipment that investigators use. Why is that? Where are people to learn how to use the different types of equipment out there? So that's where we're going to start. I feel that this book will be the first of its kind to actually help you, the investigator, know what you're doing. So when someone challenges your evidence, you can say, "I used that piece of equipment properly, so I know what I got is valid evidence."

CHAPTER FOUR

The Camera

The first piece of equipment we are going to look at is the camera. With the explosion of digital photography over the last few years, and with more and more paranormal investigators using digital cameras instead of traditional film cameras today, I thought I'd like to talk about them first. Digital cameras do have the advantage of being cheaper and, in some ways, more durable and usable than your normal film camera. They're also cheaper to use since you don't have to buy any film. Your pictures are ready right away—no film to develop. Also, most digital cameras today have A/V cables that you can connect to a TV or laptop for instant viewing.

Digital cameras, by their nature, provide an easier and quicker way than film cameras to transfer pictures from the camera to a PC for editing, enhancement, and, most importantly, analysis. Also, with memory chips or cards, you can store a lot of images. They can hold hundreds, or even thousands, of photos. Furthermore, since the card is reusable an infinite number of times, you can take as many pictures as you need to take. There should be no excuse for not being able to take enough pictures during an investigation.

Most newer digital cameras have some built-in sensitivity to infrared light. Other models can be modified for infrared (IR) photography. (Note: Such modifications will probably void your warranty.) Almost all investigators believe paranormal phenomena are more easily photographed using IR light than normal visible light because that is the spectrum in which investigators believe ghosts are visible. Finally, the cameras themselves keep improving in quality and features. Some cameras are as small and slim as a shirt pocket. Many are now also weatherproof, which helps with the outdoor investigations. Others are still full-size and professional grade. All are loaded with a wide range of features and other tools to help with your photography under a variety of conditions.

Of course, there are some drawbacks to digital cameras as well. The biggest is the technology itself. Digital cameras are marvels of technology and software. When you push the shutter button, a complex optical enhancement of the image of the object you're pointing at is made. The optical enhancement algorithms scrub the image to enhance clarity; thus, any undue movement or shaking is negated and your shot is made the best it can be. The bottom line on all this technical speak is that the image produced by a digital camera isn't the real image; it's the camera's interpretation of what it sees.

That's great for regular photography; however, for the paranormal investigator, it can be a hindrance. The very software that is designed to enhance and improve your picture-taking ability can also over enhance the picture. The camera can enhance what might only be a pinpoint of light to such a degree that it appears to be an orb.

Digital cameras rely entirely on their battery to operate. It is important to have a ready supply of fresh batteries on hand, especially during an investigation. (This theme will be brought up several times during this book.) A digital camera can really suck up battery power when hundreds of pictures are being taken, especially with a flash. Also, batteries have been known to be drained by paranormal activity.

Digital photos have a little more of a credibility gap since they can more easily be manipulated and touched up than a film picture. And digital cameras, because of the ongoing advancement of technology, can quickly become obsolete. This applies not just to the cameras but also to the memory cards they use and the software and systems for moving images from the camera to the PC.

Traditional film-style cameras still have a strong presence in the paranormal field. Typically, 35mm cameras using film with a speed between ISO 400 and ISO 800 are most common for the paranormal field. They don't have to be large, expensive, fancy cameras. Even a one-time-use disposable camera is a highly effective tool. Film has the advantage of producing a negative that can be analyzed and enhanced. The credibility of film images is higher than that of digital images since the negative can be analyzed for hoax or fraud. And with a negative, enlargements are easier to produce and result in a clearer image.

The film camera itself is more "objective" than the digital camera. There is no software to enhance a film image. The film medium simply captures the light that comes in through the lens. A dot is a dot; a bright light is a bright light. It just records what is there. Therefore, it is hard to dismiss a possible paranormal image taken with a film camera as simply the result of technology. Film cameras can also use infrared film to capture images in the IR spectrum. IR photography is, however, much more expensive, as it requires IR-capable cameras, special film, and special developing.

As with digital cameras, film cameras also have their drawbacks. Film itself can be damaged by mishandling and exposure to heat or radiation. And while uncommon, damage can result from the film development process. Similarly, any unusual or potentially paranormal images captured might be the result of a fault in the development process. Sometimes film is improperly loaded into a camera and the mistake isn't noticed until after the pictures are developed. It is entirely possible to run out of film during an investigation. The camera itself can cause a false image if there is a crack in the lens or body that lets even the slightest amount of light in—even in the dark with a flash. Finally, film pictures have to be scanned in order to be loaded onto a PC for enhancement and analysis. While scanners today are significantly better than in years past, some loss of quality is inevitable, as is contamination from dust and fingerprints.

Because of the advancement of technology, a brand-new tool has seen an increase in popularity in the field of paranormal investigating. This is the full-spectrum camera. This camera can film in the entire light spectrum, from ultraviolet (UV) to IR. Normally these cameras are in the form of a camcorder, which we will discuss later. Before I talk about the camera itself, let's take a look at the different light sources that are out there. All three are important to a paranormal investigator. UV means ultraviolet, or "beyond violet," and is not visible with the naked eye. It is found in sunlight and is what causes health issues like sunburn and certain types of cancer. Another name for UV light is black light.

IR means infrared or "below red," and again, it is not visible with the naked eye. Another name for IR is night vision. IR technology has been used in the movie industry. It's also used in the military for night-vision goggles. The light that we humans can see is called white light. This is the stuff we see with our own eyes and is only a fraction of the entire light spectrum.

These full-spectrum cameras are a very important tool. They block out the white light and only film in the UV and IR spectra. The images from a full-spectrum camera appear in "purple screen," looking like a night shot with a purplish tint. It's thought that ghosts or spirits reside in either the UV or IR spectrum, so this kind of camera can really enhance your evidence gathering. As of right now, I don't know of any downside except maybe cost with a full-spectrum camera.

As for taking an actual picture, make sure to avoid shiny surfaces when taking your photos. The shine from a glossy tombstone or pane of glass can cause anomalies that appear to look like a ghost mist, fog, or orb shapes. Never try taking photos through a glass window. It's just as easy to create shapes that aren't really there. Make sure your camera lens is clean at all times. Again, this can cause an anomalous type of image to appear. If the lens has a smudge, it can look like an anomaly. So look for that sign; try to keep your lens spotless.

Make sure you know where your camera strap and lens cover are at all times. These can appear as a vortex or ghostly images if left to dangle free from the camera. If your thumb or finger is in the way of the lens, it can cause this same effect. Make sure long hair is tied back. Hair can also appear as a ghostly anomaly. Strands of hair can look like orbs in motion as well as ghost energy.

Completely avoid taking pictures outside when conditions are windy, foggy, rainy, dusty, snowy, or when moisture is in the air. All of these conditions can cause images to appear to look like orbs. In cold weather, make sure your breath is not affecting your photos. To avoid this, do not take photos in the direction of the sun. Also, never take a picture in the direction of any light source. Preferably, have all light sources away from you or even behind you when snapping your photos.

This might sound a little silly, but talk to the ghost. When you enter an area that you want to photograph, such as a cemetery or a dwelling, follow these easy steps: Walk around the area for about ten to fifteen minutes before doing anything else. As you're walking around, clear your mind and think of only good thoughts. (Ghosts can sense your feelings and presumably read your thoughts.) After the ten to fifteen minutes, recite the following or something similar: "Hi, my name is _____. We have come here to take some pictures of you and any other ghosts/spirits that are here in order to show and document that there is life after death. We have only the best of intentions. We are not here to do any harm, and we will only be here long enough to use some of our equipment that we have brought to prove that you exist, and then we will leave. Our only request is to take a picture of any of you that are here. Thank you so much. I'll be taking pictures now. Thanks."

When taking your photos inside, you want to do the same thing as outside. Make sure to avoid shiny surfaces. It is common for the shine from a glossy countertop, wall, pane of glass, etc., to cause anomalies that appear to look like ghost mist, fog, and orb shapes. Take all the pictures you think you need to and whatever else you're going to use during your investigation, and then get out. On the way out, stop one last time and say, "Thank you so much for putting up with me and my team or group. We enjoyed being here in your company and are very grateful for any photos you have allowed us to have of you. Thanks again."

Most ghost energy will appear in the air from two to ten feet above the ground, so focus a portion of your attention at that level, but don't limit yourself totally to it. Ghostly phenomena can and will also appear above your head at times, so be sure to snap some random shots up above at times. Note: In a building, ghostly phenomena can appear at any level of the structure and at any height.

The odds of encountering an evil spirit or entity are slim, but here is a little advice. Don't go hunting for evil spirits or entities. *Do not* dare them to come around. If you hear or see a sign of evil spirits, get out; leave immediately. You are not trained to handle these evil spirits or entities. Only a person or group that is trained in handling evil spirits should go up against them. I will say this several more times in this book. I will emphasize this until I'm blue in the face. You are only going to create trouble you don't want. Trust me on this!

Now back to camera procedures. Try following your instincts when taking ghost photos. If you have a psychic/medium in your group (I feel that you should), take pictures around that person, especially if the psychic/medium reports that he or she feels a presence. Remember, the purpose is to catch anomalies and people together in the same photo. Here's another trick to use when ghosts might be following you around: put the camera over your shoulder and snap a picture behind you. This can be a very effective technique at times. Again, trust me on this.

Remember your flash limitations also. A flash can only be useful for up to a certain distance; normally it is fifteen feet. So if you are in, say, a cemetery at night and take a picture of a mausoleum or a gravestone thirty feet or more away, the image will be hard to view. It could also be a bit washed out, as well as any anomalies present. (*Important note:* the flash will help highlight the anomaly if the background image is within the fifteen-foot range.) Use a flash attachment to help you increase your range.

As I said earlier, I am going to tell you some ways to narrow the skeptics. When it comes to orbs, there are many ways to debunk an orb, so here's an idea to try to validate the orbs you get shots of. You should use two, or even three, digital or film cameras of the same model, and either a wireless or wired remote control (I think the wireless works best because it's less cumbersome). Set the cameras each on a tripod, and put them in the same room but at different angles or locations. You should make sure that all the cameras will cover each other, meaning that all of them will overlap, giving you the same shot but from a different viewpoint.

Using a remote system that you can buy and hook up to your cameras, you can take pictures at the same time. As I said earlier, one of the debunking themes that are commonly used about orbs is that it's a smudge on the camera lens itself, the result of inclement weather, a drop of water on the lens, or a bug. Well, if there are two or three shots of an orb from two or three different cameras at the same time, it's hard to debunk it that way. The chances of having a smudge or a drop of moisture at the exact same angle on all the cameras are astronomical. Also, if it's a moving orb and all the cameras capture it as its moving from three different angles, again, it's hard to debunk.

Here's another one using the same setup but including the human factor. This is a rarity, but it is more common if some of your team members are mediums—and I will talk about this later in the book. As you're taking these pictures and your team is doing their normal investigation in the room and you hear one of your members say that he or she was just touched and that same moment you record on all your cameras that an orb or orbs were near or touching that particular member at the same time, to me that is proof that that orb could have been one of a spiritual nature. You now have two separate pieces of evidence from the same time, with which you can prove that something out of the normal happened. It could be paranormal.

It is hard for a scientific person to debunk these two methods when I have that kind of information. I'm sure there are other ideas out there that people can come up with to help debunk the debunkers. This is another reason we should all be working together as one, not separate and hiding our ideas and methods like it's a top-secret plan to take over the world.

Recommended Digital Cameras for Paranormal Photography

If you're still overwhelmed by the number of cameras available, the following list highlights several models that have been field-tested with excellent results:

- All Kodak EasyShare models (6 megapixels or higher)
- HP Photosmart R937
- Canon EOS-10D
- Nikon D3 Digital SLR (This camera features one of the highest ISO settings currently on the market!)
- Nikon COOLPIX P80

CHAPTER FIVE

The Camcorder

Another tool that we use during investigations is a handheld camcorder on a tripod. During an investigation, we attempt to capture visual data proving that something paranormal exists, and camcorders are one tool we use to do that. There are many types, brands, and models of camcorders used by paranormal teams. We have a Sony DXG 581V HD model, but there are quite a few others out there. The most important feature that any camcorder needs when used during an investigation is the ability to film in darkness, or night-vision capabilities. We will discuss lux ratings a little more in a bit. Since most of a paranormal investigation is conducted in the dark, this feature is the most critical by far.

Secondly, you must decide if you want one with an internal hard drive, DVD, or tape as the storage media. Again, the type you get is based on your preference and what you can afford. We like the ones with internal hard drives so that we don't have to swap out tapes or the DVD every thirty to sixty minutes. Ours also has a memory card in it. We have a 16GB card, and this makes for hours of recording. It also makes it easier to copy video to other media or computers. Even though we use the cameras with full-spectrum technology, we still use an external IR light so that we can capture images at a greater distance. The standard camera can tape only about twenty to thirty feet in the dark. With an external IR light, you can extend that distance to sixty feet or farther, depending on the light used.

So what is lux? A lux is a unit of measure of luminance (light) in a given area. The simple way to put it is to say that the lux refers to the amount of light that is visibly present. In order to record video in the dark, a camera should have a rating of 0 lux.

With all devices, there are positives and negatives. One negative we have found with a few of the camcorder cameras is that they are very sensitive and pick up a lot of airborne debris that other cameras, or the naked eye, will not. Some of the cameras pick up these airborne particles and make them appear larger, more solid, and, in some cases, glowing. This results in data that has to be reviewed more closely just to confirm that it is nothing more than dust. That is called a false positive. An example of a type of camera that does this is JVC cameras with an external light. So with all technology, know what you want and how you want to use it. Understanding the technology is the key to purchasing the right tool for the job at hand.

When setting up your video recorder, make sure it is firmly on a tripod (if one is being used) and that the night-vision feature is enabled. Don't hold it in your hands. I don't care who you are; you will not be able to hold the camera steady enough to film great pictures. Your hands will shake, and this will create problems with your recording. Make sure there is no one smoking and that everyone participating remains still. During the recording, it is a good idea to take a couple of short video recordings, making sure that the straps and other attachments are removed from the camera. Be sure you are using the IR light or full-spectrum light if it is nighttime, and that the photographer's hair is completely pulled back and out of the way, so as not to interfere with the image produced.

Keep video cameras recording throughout the investigation. Place stationary recorders in the areas of reported activity. I also like to place passive infrared motion detectors in the reported activity area. Outfit investigators with handheld recorders, and instruct them to keep the recorders on at all times. This is to give you a constant diary of where everyone is during an investigation so that if you do get something anomalous during your investigation, you can cross-check to see where your investigators are during that time to make sure they weren't the ones causing the anomaly. Make sure investigators have extra batteries so the recordings are uninterrupted and functional and investigators can document everything happening during the investigation.

Passive infrared motion detectors are a useful tool for ghost hunters. They work great when left in a room during the time when no investigator is present. We have had them go off in rooms where no activity has been reported, and upon further investigation, we found some great evidence of spirit activity in the area. I'll talk more about these episodes shortly.

Now, before you ever do a review of evidence, you need to play with your recorder and know how it works when it comes to uploading your evidence to a TV or PC. When we got our DXG full spectrum, I read the manual and looked at the camera and thought I had it down. A week later, we went out on a fun investigation to one of my favorite places in the Fresno area, called Fresno Flats, in Oakhurst. I was able to record with no problem. The problem came when I attempted to download the video to my PC. I didn't know how the program in the camera itself uploaded to the PC. I hit the wrong button and lost the whole video. Talk about an embarrassment. Good thing it was a fun investigation and not a client's case. I had to go back to the manual, get over my ego, and learn how to actually upload the video properly.

Also, a lot of times when we do evidence review, we like to go to each other's houses to do it and have a buffet-style dinner or lunch while doing it. When you go, though, make sure you have all the cords that you need to do the upload. It's pretty embarrassing to get ready to watch your evidence and find you don't have the cords to do it. I learned that lesson the hard way too.

My recommendation for a type of camcorder is that you can buy any model, really. Just make sure it's got night vision—or better yet, get a full-spectrum; that will alleviate any problems, period.

Recommended Types of Camcorders for Use in Investigations

- Sony HD Digital Camcorder
- Sony DXG 581 Full-Spectrum HD

There are others, of course, but these two are what I personally recommend.

CHAPTER SIX

Dowsing Rods and Pendulums

Dowsing rods, in theory, use the energy that surrounds them; supposedly, the presence of an energy source will make them either cross or uncross. At an investigation, the user should hold them out, one in each hand, very steadily. If they cross, get whichever one of your members that is holding the EMF meter at the time to check the energy level around the rods. It is considered paranormal activity when they cross. The more they cross, the more energy is purported to be present.

A pendulum is an object (usually a crystal or another natural stone or pendant) placed at the end of a string, rope, or chain that is used to receive answers to questions. Some claim that messages received by this process, called dowsing, come from the "higher self" and can help people to answer questions beyond the normal five senses. Dowsing answers yes-or-no questions and locates people or objects on a map or underground in a paranormal investigation. Test your pendulum in a quiet, calming space. Stand upright with your body completely balanced. Hold the pendulum a foot or two in front of your face. Breathe deeply and calmly. Try to ground yourself by feeling your weight and feet on the ground. Feel your energy going from the top of your head, connecting you to both the spirit and the ground. Do this until you feel absolutely calm and ready to ask a question.

Ask your pendulum to show you "yes." The pendulum's movement should be clearly in one direction. Tell the pendulum "Thank you," and wait for it to slow to a stop. Ask the pendulum to show you "no." Thank it when the direction is clear. Allow it to come to a standstill. Ask your pendulum a yes-or-no question that you know the answer to. Try this over several days at different times of the day. If the pendulum is correct around 75 percent of the time, then it is ready for use in paranormal studies. If it is incorrect, go through the process of grounding again. Try to calm your mind with deep breathing, and ask the pendulum again.

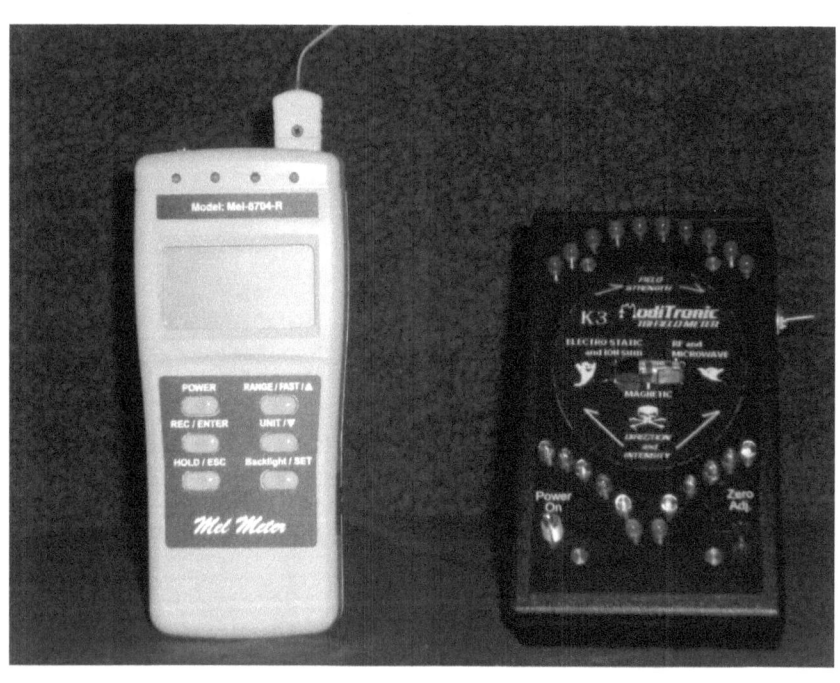

CHAPTER SEVEN

The EMF Detector

M ichael Persinger, professor of psychology at Laurentian University, Ontario, Canada, has a theory, which he presents in a chapter of the book *Hauntings and Poltergeists* (McFarland & Co, 2001), that the sensation commonly associated with having a paranormal experience is merely a side effect of both sides of our brain trying to work together. Simplified, the idea goes like this: When the right hemisphere of the brain, the side associated with emotion, is stimulated in a particular part of the cerebral region, and then the left hemisphere, the language side, is called upon to make sense of these stimulations, the mind generates a sense of presence. Dr. Persinger believes things such as apparitions, ghost lights, poltergeist activity, and so on are caused by the natural electrical magnetic field that the earth creates, which, if powerful enough, can trick our brain into seeing or hearing things. Okay, that's the scientist version of what an EMF is. Now let me give you another.

The electromagnetic field (EMF) meter was originally designed to locate man-made sources of electric and magnetic radiation and to offer a reading of the relative strength (and direction, if you are a skilled and competent operator) of the EM field. Natural (as opposed to man-made) EM fields rarely fluctuate and require a geomagnetometer (a very expensive gadget in a paranormal investigator's kit) to measure them properly.

Paranormal investigators often have a couple of EMF meters in their investigation kits and use them for a variety of reasons. The most favored theory is the theory that a high-level EMF suggests a ghost is present. Paranormal researchers will often take baseline readings of a supposedly haunted building. They will often measure things like the temperature and the electromagnetic field in each room or area. Then, during the rest of the investigation, they will continue to take readings to see if they rise or fall in the different areas, and they make note of such fluctuations.

These fluctuations are often attributed to spiritual energy manifesting itself or are, at least, noted as odd. However, unless you take these baseline tests and monitor the EMF levels in the building over a long period of time, it's impossible to be able to know if a reading is anomalous or not. Also, magnetic fields are physical fields produced by electrically charged objects. The electric field is produced by stationary charges, and the magnetic field by moving charges or currents.

EMF is often described as being a static field—one that does not change or fluctuate over time. Thus, a suddenly higher reading must be anomalous. In fact, EMFs do change over time, but they do so very slowly. When fluctuations in an EMF are detected at locations that are reputed to be haunted, it is more likely and probable that the fluctuation is being caused by items in the building that are electronic or things that are electrically or magnetically charged, rather than by the spirits of the dead. One way to reduce this possibility is, if possible, to have all the electricity turned off during the investigation; or, at the least, to have the major electrical appliances turned off. This will make any questionable readings more paranormal than electrical.

Experience-inducing fields (EIFs) are simply fields that have experience-inducing properties. Current evidence suggests that EIFs are varying magnetic fields with low frequency and a moderate intensity/amplitude. EIFs overlay any existing ambient and static magnetic field present in any certain area. This would probably be the geomagnetic field itself (the magnetic field that is constantly present at the earth's surface, which we are subject to continuously), which is considered to be static but actually does change over long periods of time.

Solar flares and solar winds can have major effects on the

geomagnetic field, depending on the sun's day-to-day activity. Also, these types of magnetic fields are not considered to be very important in inducing hallucinations in any way, and EIFs, if present, would most likely appear as fluctuations on top of the local static field. EIFs are not caused by or contributed to by household appliances that are powered with electricity from DC or AC current, specifically the 110/220 AC current supplied to many homes. EIFs also do not cause people to hallucinate when they have been exposed to high levels of EIFs for a long period of time. Only around 25 percent of the population shows an increased susceptibility, and this is usually due to increased neuronal instability in certain regions of the brain. This is another theory that ghost researchers use and another reason they use EMF meters on their investigations; however, it's also worth noting that these EIFs are not detectable with a standard EMF meter.

Before using the EMF meter on an investigation, become familiar with how it works. Hold the meter at arm's length and walk around your own home, taking initial readings around sources such as lights and electrical outlets. Most units come with a manual that lists most household and major appliances and their corresponding electromagnetic readings. When using EMF detection meters, it is important to make a series of baseline measurements in order to highlight any unusual readings. A normal range of readings is between 0.1 to 10 mG (milligauss), though some locations may have higher man-made sources. If you are close to domestic appliances, the reading can exceed 30 mG.

Most meters on the market are handheld, and this is not really ideal. To use them properly, make sure you *stand still!* Or better yet, put them down when doing a long reading—say during an EVP session. Even moving around can affect the readout slightly, and unless you know this, you may be incorrectly interpreting your data. In an ideal world, you would purchase a triaxial EMF meter as opposed to the single-axis meter that currently dominates the market. Both varieties have their uses in investigations, since a single-axis meter is generally a better tool for locating the source of an emission. A triaxial meter, however, can be less static, and the data can be recorded onto its memory or fed directly into a computer. It takes out possible human error.

Here are some other pointers. When investigating, scan the area you are investigating with a swaying motion from side to side *very slowly,* as well as up and down—not at the same time, though. Too many times I see investigators doing readings, and they're just swinging the EMF meter all around like they're drunk or something, especially if they think they're detecting a spirit. All this does is give you a false reading. Do this in a *gentle* and *even* pattern. Never jerk the meter into position. Note: If you are using the TriField Natural EM meter, you will need to be extra gentle, because it is especially sensitive to movement

Spirit phenomena will normally register in the range of 2.0 to 7.0 mG. Note: For those that are using the TriField meters, you will want to use the SUM setting for detecting ghosts. If after eliminating any power sources in that range you are still getting a steady reading, you probably have detected an anomaly that could be a spirit. When scanning a room, be sure to check the furniture. This should include such things as the couch and chairs. Like I said earlier, one of the solidifying things that got me into the field was when the chair in my house turned a full forty-five degrees toward me when I asked if there was anyone there. That's right; believe it or not, ghosts do sit down— not that they need to, but they do all the same. The same applies outdoors with benches, porch swings, and things of that nature. It's best to have one person scanning with a meter while another is close by with a camera. When something is detected, the cameraperson can be notified and pictures immediately taken. Again, this helps with the validation of your evidence. If you can always have more than one piece of evidence to support an event, it's more difficult to debunk. If you can get three pieces, such as an EVP, picture or video, and some EMF readings all at the time, it's hard to debunk. I don't care what the doubters say; that's just too many coincidences occurring at the same time.

A lot of teams don't do this, but it really helps: be sure to mark active areas with brightly colored nonreflective tape. (This is where you should also put your passive motion-detector camera. If something happens, the motion camera will hopefully pick it up.) Do this so that you can recheck these areas later in the investigation. This is done for two reasons: (1) areas that register activity are usually frequented by spirits and should be considered a hot spot for your studies, and (2) it is also important to recheck these areas in case it's just an electrical reading. If continued checks reveal high readings, then it's most likely electrical related, because spirits are not going to stay in one place for too long. They are constantly moving. Finally, don't be frightened when the meter sounds. That's why you're there! Enjoy the moment.

If you're using a K2 meter, you can use it not only for checking for EMF fields but also for communication. To do this, we try to get the spirit to light up the LED lights. The most common way is to ask the spirit yes-or-no questions. When you ask the spirit these questions, ask it to light two lights for yes and one for no.

To use the meter, first hold down the button on the front of the meter to turn it on. Make sure you point and scan the area for any variations in the magnetic field. If you get a reading, try to locate where the reading is coming from. The range of the meter's sensitivity is 0 to 20 mG. The effective range from the meter to the active field is usually from zero to about six feet max.

Normal activity on this type of meter is 0 to 2 mG. It's purported that paranormal activity is between 3 and 10 mG. Anything above ten is most likely not paranormal. It takes too much energy for a spirit to manifest past the 10 mG range. I am not saying it can't happen, but it's beyond a spirit's capability, according to all my research.

Chapter Eight

Digital Video Recorder (DVR) System

As paranormal investigators, we are constantly in search of data to show that the paranormal does exist or, at the very least, to answer some very important questions that a lot of people, both those in the paranormal field and those not, want to know. There are a lot of techniques used to record evidence of the paranormal, and using video is one of them. Using a digital video recorder with an external infrared camera attached to it really helps you record multiple places at once without having to be there. The DVR systems used are very similar to those used in department stores and convenience stores for security purposes. The main difference is that those systems connect the cameras in a permanent stationary position, whereas most paranormal investigators use tripod systems to create temporary stationary systems.

The cameras that most teams use are of the day/night variety, so that they can record both in daylight and, especially, at night. There are many different types and styles of video cameras. Some can film up to eighty feet, while others can film all the way up to two hundred feet. Keep in mind, though, that you don't want too many long-range cameras if you are doing home investigations. The smaller rooms will cause what I call "the wash-out effect" on the walls.

The cameras are connected in two different ways, depending on the size of location that you're recording. For smaller areas, you can go wireless. For larger areas, you can use cables. The type of IR camera setup cable will depend on the type of DVR and the distance from the cameras to the DVR. These cables come in various lengths from twenty-five to three hundred feet. I prefer the one-hundred-foot length because it's easier to manage and I haven't found a real need for anything longer.

We use tripods in various styles and sizes also. We have some that sit on a table that are seven inches high, and we have others that are as high as fifty-six inches. We also have some that are very flexible and have legs that can be wrapped around a stationary item.

While recording, make announcements as you enter and leave rooms, so you can track your progress through the place you're investigating. That way you can have an easier time during evidence review. I know I don't always remember where I am or what room I was in ten minutes after I've left the room; also, the team member doing the evidence review might be someone other than the person who made the recordings. Making announcements alleviates the headache of figuring out where the recording is from. When you set up the cameras, try to put them in a corner and make them about shoulder high. That way the cameras can record the whole room.

Chapter Nine

The Famous EVP

M ost people today use the digital recorder for their electronic voice phenomena detection. In the early days, most used an analog, or tape, recorder, but such recorders emit mechanical noises. The sounds from motors, tape movement, etc. can overlap the actual EVP that you're trying to capture. This common problem, however, can be overcome by using an external microphone. Just extend the microphone as far as possible from the recorder itself. Another problem with analog recording equipment is the quality of the recordings it produces. You can't use computer software to boost the sound level without distorting the recording.

For digital recorders, I recommend that you use the highest quality setting that your recorder has. This allows for the best post investigation editing possible. Keep in mind, though, that most recorders will drop some data in order to save space. This means that the recorder will delete some higher- or lower-pitched noises that are very short in duration. When a recording is converted from the proprietary format of the digital recorder to a more standard computer format, such as a .wav file, the conversion will limit the amount of quality loss. Some researchers recommend using the external microphone even with a digital recorder. I personally don't think this is necessary.

The birth of the famous EVP (electronic voice phenomena) can be attributed to Thomas Edison because of his phonograph and recording inventions. Thomas Edison was known to be involved in the spiritualist movement that was popular in the US and abroad in the late '20s and '30s, near the end of his life. Edison experimented with a spirit communication machine, which he did not name as far as I could determine in my research. Unfortunately, he died in 1931 before he could document any results from the machine. The machine itself is in the Smithsonian museum in Washington, DC.

In 1959, a man named Friedrich Juergenson, a Swedish artist and film producer, noticed that there were unexplained voices on recordings he had made of songbirds in the woods. He continued his research and wrote a book entitled *Voices from the Universe*, (Rymden, Saxon-Lindstrom, 1964.) In 1982, a woman named Sarah Estep from Severna Park, MD, began the American Association for Electronic Voice Phenomena (EVP) with the intent to prove that there is life beyond the physical plane. Her research began as an attempt to contact her departed husband. In the same year, Sarah published a book entitled *Voices of Eternity*, (Mass Market Paperback, July, 1988) in which she wrote about her fifteen years of EVP research. She retired from doing active investigating around 2000. As far I know, she never was able to contact her husband.

What exactly is an EVP? Well, no one knows for sure, but there are a lot of theories out there. The simplest explanation I can put together for you is EVPs are unknown sounds or voices, for which there is no logical or intelligible explanation, which appear on electronic recordings. One theory on EVP states that the voices are projections of the person recording; another states that the voices are a residual haunting and not really a spirit: when a traumatic event happens on a site, the environment absorbs the energy associated with the event and merely replays the same events over and over. Yet another theory claims that the sounds are extraterrestrial. The one I tend to believe in the most is that the sounds or voices are the sounds of spirits who are attempting to contact the physical world. Some people claim that EVPs are answers to questions posed by the investigators recording. At one of my favorite places to investigate, the Zalud House in Porterville, California, I get great EVPs that answer direct questions.

Before I even go into explaining about how to do an EVP session, let's start off by saying that we are all in agreement that ghosts were once people, and that, for whatever reason, they remained earthbound after they died. With that having been said, would it not be safe to say that a ghost is no less intelligent than its former self? In fact, I would argue that once ghosts have moved on to the next plane of existence, they are actually smarter, because they no longer have earthly limitations put on them. Bottom line: ghosts don't become stupid when they become ghosts. This brings me again to my least favorite topic: *provocation*.

The subject of provocation is a hot topic with me, as you will soon know. I've written a few articles about this very subject on a site called United Paranormal International. The UPI site is a great place to learn more about the paranormal field without being harassed or ridiculed about your ideas or opinions. Too many people use provocation in their investigations and get themselves into serious trouble that they don't know how to get out of.

Provocation came from the clergy and certain types of religious investigators called demonologists. It is used to make demons show themselves in order that the demonologist can gather enough evidence to get the church involved. Only properly trained people from the church or people trained by the church should be doing this. Unfortunately, today it's used by groups or individuals on famous TV shows, and everyone thinks it's cool. It's not, and like I said before, it can get you into trouble that you don't know how to or want to handle.

A paranormal group or investigator usually will provoke by making fun of a demon, demanding that it show itself, or, even worse, using foul language. However, there is a major difference between the clergy/demonologist and you. If a demonologist is attacked by an entity, he or she knows how to handle it. *You don't*. Now, with that having been said, very rarely are you going to run into a demonic spirit. I'm not saying that it won't happen—it could. But you can piss off a human spirit also by teasing it or telling it that it's stupid, etc. I've been to a Para conference where this actually happened. It was a human spirit that got mad at being made fun of and attacked the provoker, and she started feeling really sick and dizzy and, once taken out from the building, asked what had happened.

For a paranormal team or person to provoke whatever is in the premises is not only foolish but also extremely dangerous. Many investigators have learned the hard way. Even some of the famous ones have had their own problems. It looks great on TV, but behind the scenes, these people have some serious personal issues that you might not know about. Remember, like I said earlier, ghosts used to be regular people like you and me when they were alive. So provoking is just not needed. Got it? I hope so.

One thing that you may have to remember is that even though ghosts may have been human at one time like you and me, most are from an earlier time frame. Because of this, especially if you're at a place that has never been investigated before, you might have to teach them about the equipment that you're using—what it does and what you want them to do with it. This, I feel, will enhance your evidence gathering and make it all the more easy. Tell them what the EMF reader is and how it works. Tell them that they need to come near it and that if they touch it, it will give off a sound that you can hear. When using a voice recorder, tell them to speak into it so that you can hear it. This helps us to communicate with them. You'll be surprised how much evidence you get that way, although it might take a couple of times going back to a given site to actually get something. As they get more comfortable with the equipment and you, you'll get more and more evidence. This is what happens when we go to the Zalud House. Only once have we been there and not gotten great grade-A EVPs. And the one time we didn't, guess why. Yep, we had a new person provoke the spirits and piss them off, so they just shut down.

Well, now you're probably asking yourself, "What kind of questions do I need or want to ask a spirit?" There are many different kinds of questions that you can ask. Be creative; don't ask the same boring questions over and over again. I know one couple who ask the same questions in the same order on every investigation they conduct. I can almost tell what they're going to ask before they ask it.

So what questions should you ask? You're likely to get one- or two-word answers. It's a rarity when you get a full-sentence answer. So you will want to ask questions that will entice those one- or two-word answers. Also, always allow ten to fifteen seconds between your questions. It takes a lot of energy for spirits to answer even one word. Below are some great questions that will make you look like you know what you're doing not only to the spirits but also to your fellow investigators. The following questions are in no discernible order, but you can use your imagination as to which would come first. And there are many more that I'm sure you can come up with on your own.

EVP Questions

1. Is there anyone here that would like to talk to us?
2. Can you tell us your name?
3. How old are you?
4. Why are you here?
5. Are you sad or angry?
6. Are you alone?
7. How many of you are here?
8. What year is it?
9. Can you see us?
10. What do we look like?
11. Do you know my name?
12. Can we help you?
13. Do you need our help?
14. Are you afraid of where you are?
15. Do you have something to tell us?
16. Do you have any pets with you?
17. What kind of clothes are you wearing?
18. How many fingers am I holding up?
19. Are you married?
20. How long have you been married?
21. What year did you get married?
22. What is your husband's/wife's name?
23. Is he/she with you?
24. Did you have any children?
25. Are they with you?
26. How many did you have?
27. Do you rest here?
28. Are you here all the time?

29. Are there any children here?
30. Do you like being here alone when we leave?
31. Where should we take our investigation next?

Depending on what the answer is, the last question in the list could be a bad question or a good question. Take anything the spirit says in response to this question under scrutiny. Don't ignore the warning signs if the spirit wants you to go somewhere alone. Take a fellow investigator with you at all times. The spirit could be trying to steer you to a place where it is stronger and has more control. When we get to the actual investigating, I'll talk more about how to do an EVP session itself. For now, let's move on to the next piece of equipment.

CHAPTER TEN

EM Pump

You may have seen an EM pump used on some of the paranormal shows. What you might not know is what it is and how it works. An EM pump is a device that creates electromagnetic energy and disperses it into the room it is placed in. It is thought that electromagnetic fields give entities energy that they need to manifest themselves; the higher the electromagnetic field, the higher the possibility the spirit will manifest itself. In fact, not only can an EM pump give entities the energy they need to manifest themselves, but it can also help prevent the power in batteries from being drained. This is why I constantly harp about having plenty of batteries with you during your investigations—the spirits will supposedly use the energy from your batteries to gain the strength to manifest themselves.

Many times, investigators may find that in cases where there are a lot of entities trying to communicate all at once, their batteries will drain very quickly on all their equipment that runs on batteries. The EM pump will help to alleviate this problem. It will give the spirits the energy they need and save the battery life of the equipment that the investigators use. When you use the EM pump, set the device where you are trying to capture audio and video evidence. Don't set the EMF meter directly on or near the pump, because you could damage it.

Note: Keep your EMF meters at least a foot away from the pump, because they could damage it. Yes, I repeated myself, but I want to make sure you get that point. The last thing you want to do is destroy an expensive piece of equipment.

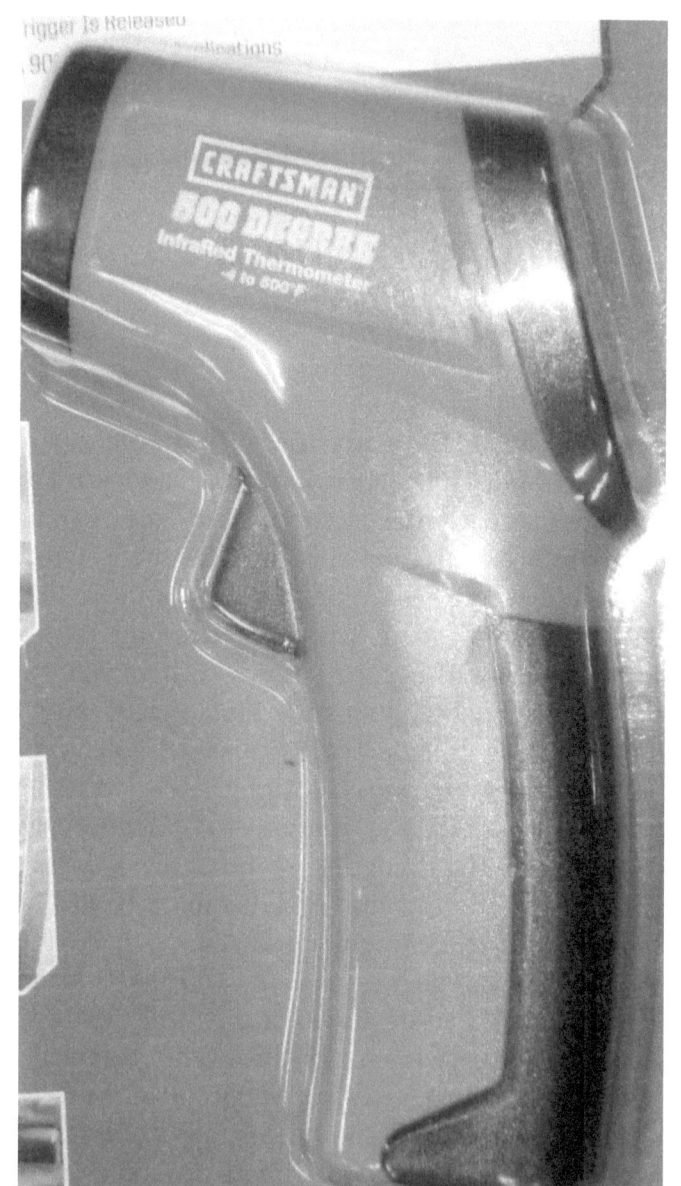

CHAPTER ELEVEN

Thermometers

Very often, paranormal investigators will notice unexplained temperature fluctuations during an investigation. When these fluctuations occur, an investigator's first priority should be to look for any natural occurrences for the change in temperature. For example, you might check to see if the air conditioning has turned on, or if someone has opened a door or a window. Sometimes older buildings can be drafty, and sudden gusts of wind can occur inside the building. Once natural causes for the temperature change have been eliminated, then the next task at hand should be to document the fluctuation. Otherwise, it is nothing more than a subjective observation.

Using a thermometer to document temperature changes is a simple process, but it depends on the investigator using the correct type of thermometer for the situation at hand and knowing how to interpret the results. There are two primary types of thermometers used in paranormal investigations: ambient and infrared.

Ambient Thermometers

An ambient thermometer's job is to measure the temperature of whatever it comes into contact with (the air, your hand, etc.). Older ambient thermometers used a glass tube containing mercury. Most new ambient thermometers are digital.

Digital Thermometers

A digital thermometer does not contain mercury, but rather relies on an electronic component called a thermistor. A thermistor is basically an electronic resistor that is temperature sensitive. At low temperatures, a thermistor will have a high level of resistance, which will prevent it from conducting electricity very well. As the temperature increases, the thermistor's conductivity improves. The thermometer's manufacturer calibrates the thermistor by measuring its resistance at various temperatures. A simple computer within the thermometer uses this information to calculate the thermistor's temperature based on its level of electronic resistance.

Working with a Digital Thermometer
If you are going to be using a digital thermometer for paranormal investigations, then you need to know where the thermistor is located. This is important, because it is actually the thermistor that measures the temperature. If you carry a digital thermometer by its thermistor, then the only measurement that you will take is the temperature of your hand.

Although all digital thermometers work in about the same way, some are better suited to paranormal investigations than others. If you are shopping for a digital thermometer to use for paranormal research, then the two main things that you should be looking for are a fast response time and an exposed thermistor. An exposed thermistor can be used as a temperature probe. If you feel a cold spot, you should be able to insert the thermistor into the middle of the cold spot, and the thermometer should be responsive enough to instantly report the cold spot's temperature.

Infrared Thermometers
Infrared thermometers work based on the principle that any object with a temperature above absolute zero (zero Kelvin, -273.16° C, or -459.69° F) radiates infrared energy. The heat within an object causes molecular vibrations. These vibrations in turn induce electron vibrations, which lead to the electromagnetic coupling that causes the infrared energy to be emitted. Because of the mechanics involved in this process, the wavelengths of the resulting infrared energy vary according to temperature. The infrared energy that is emitted from an object is a type of electromagnetic radiation

and has many of the same characteristics as light. The energy is transmitted at the speed of light and flows indefinitely in all directions.

Working with an Infrared Thermometer

Infrared thermometers are ideal for paranormal investigations because they respond to temperature changes instantly. The key to successfully using an infrared thermometer is to understand exactly what it is that you are measuring. Most infrared thermometers contain a built-in laser pointer to help the user determine which direction the thermometer is pointed in. Many people incorrectly assume that when they are using an infrared thermometer they are measuring the temperature of whatever the dot happens to be touching. While an infrared thermometer does measure the temperature of the object that it is pointed at, the accuracy of the measurement varies with distance. If you measure an object's temperature at point-blank range, then for all practical purposes the temperature that is being displayed is the object's temperature. If you measure the same object's temperature from twenty feet away, you will likely get a very different measurement. The reason this occurs is that the size of the cone that is being measured increases with distance. Therefore, you aren't just measuring the object that the thermometer is pointed at; the thermopile is also collecting infrared energy from the air between itself and the object, and you may also be collecting infrared energy from other nearby objects. In these types of situations, the thermometer may report an average temperature or a dominant temperature.

When using an infrared thermometer on an investigation, paranormal investigators should try to take measurements from as close to the target object as possible in order to ensure accuracy. It is also important to realize that an infrared thermometer is not usually capable of measuring a floating cold spot. Pointing the thermometer at a cold spot will yield the aggregate temperature of the cold spot, the air behind the cold spot, and any objects behind the cold spot. Although the thermometer might display a lower temperature when aimed at the cold spot, it is not actually displaying the cold spot's temperature; rather, what you are seeing is the cold spot's influence on the aggregate temperatures of nearby objects.

Unfortunately, there does not seem to be a single thermometer that is ideally suited to all circumstances. My recommendation is to use a combination of thermometer types during an investigation.

CHAPTER TWELVE

The Ovilus

One of the newest pieces of equipment in the paranormal toolbox is the Ovilus. Invented by Bill Chappell, the Ovilus uses environmental readings, such as electromagnetic field and temperature changes, to produce words through electronic speech synthesis.

The Ovilus has many different modes. In dictionary mode, it uses an onboard database of words connected to numbers. The environmental readings produce the number, and the Ovilus then speaks the word connected to that number. In phonetic mode, the Ovilus uses EMF variations to produce a phoneme, combinations of which create words that are not in the database.

There is also a reverse phonetic mode; a touch mode, in which the Ovilus will make a pinging sound when touched; an energy mode, in which the Ovilus acts as an electromagnetic pump; a white noise mode, in which the Ovilus produces low-volume static noise for EVP sessions; a say-last-word mode, in which the Ovilus will repeat all the words produced when it was in dictionary mode; and even a sync mode to help sync audio and video equipment.

If you are a fan of such paranormal television shows as *Ghost Adventures*, *Paranormal Challenge*, *Celebrity Ghost Hunt*, *The Haunted Collector*, *Paranormal State*, and *The Haunted*, you more than likely have seen the Ovilus in action. The show *Ghost Adventures* featured a version of the Ovilus that was equipped with a built-in night vision video camera.

Does the Ovilus work as a useful tool during EVP sessions? Can the dead really speak through it? At this time, we cannot answer that question. Some paranormal teams swear by this device, and others have stopped using it totally. Keep in mind that printed on the Ovilus itself by the manufacturer is "For entertainment purposes only." The manufacturer even lists on their website the odds of getting a relative response: 1:512 for the Ovilus I, 1:1024 for the Ovilus FX/Video Ovilus, and 1:2,048 for the PX. The odds change with the different modes also, from 1:2,048 in dictionary mode to 1:71 in phonetic mode.

For 11th Hour Paranormal, the verdict of the use of this tool for investigations is not yet in. We personally don't use it as a main tool in our investigations. At this time, we do not show any data associated with it to a client. We need to do a lot more research before that happens.

CHAPTER THIRTEEN

Trigger Objects: A Valid Investigation Technique?

rigger objects: what are they, and how do they fit into the world of paranormal investigating? A trigger object is an inanimate object such as a toy, a personal belonging of the entity you're trying to contact, or something else associated with the entity in question. These objects are used in an attempt to attract the entity's attention or to possibly capture the object in motion as a result of physical contact of the object by the entity.

Many investigators will use items like toys (e.g., stuffed animals, balls, candy, music, marbles, jacks, birthday cards, etc.) when dealing with the ghosts of children who have passed on. Because of the way a child's mind works, using a toy is a way of not only drawing the entity close to you but also of giving it confidence that you are not there to harm it in any way; instead you show them that you just want to play with them. There have been instances where an investigator has placed a small ball in a bedroom or a playroom, and then, moments later, the ball has moved. Now, to put the ball down and see if it moves is great, but it's not enough, because of contamination. The investigator must quarantine the area by both sealing off the entire room in question and making a video note of it. You also need to have a second investigator there to validate the experience.

If you're doing an experiment with everyone present, you need to make sure no one is moving and that there is no kind of airflow present; otherwise, your experiment will be contaminated. The entities of children are assumed to be playful all the time, but there have been instances where an entity of a child has been, let's say, disrespectful or mischievous and has caused some chaos in a location.

On the other hand, when dealing with an adult entity, you have to be a bit more scientific to see if you can not only appeal to their nature but also catch the possible movement on video. Theoretically, since the spirits of adults tend to bind themselves to earthly possessions, people, or places, one has to, if possible, try to associate those spirits with objects that were of a personal nature to the spirits. Examples are keys, a pen, photos, an heirloom, etc.

We were once at the Zalud House location, and it was one of the family members' birthdays. Before the investigation, I bought a birthday card for the family member. During the investigation, I said "Happy birthday" to the spirit and opened the card and read it to him. Not only did we get an EVP saying "Thank you," but the spirit also interacted with our EMF detector in answering other questions. It culminated in a great night for evidence.

Trigger objects are not only fun to use, but they also have a way of connecting you to the spirit and of allowing the spirit to see that you're not there to cause harm. So if you're not using any type of trigger object or objects in your investigations, you're missing out on a great way of getting your spirits to interact with you.

Note: There are a couple of companies that are now actually creating trigger objects, such as a toy train that a child would have played with and an old-fashioned lamp that spirits would have carried around with them before the invention of electricity. You can actually find some of them at the Ghost Hunters store online.

CHAPTER FOURTEEN

Types of Spirits

L et's talk about some of the different types of spirits that you might run into during an investigation. When you run into something out there, you'll need to figure out what it was. One of the things you will run into is what investigators call shadow people. There's a growing interest in the phenomenon of shadow people. What are they—ghosts, interdimensional beings, time travelers, or something else?

"What was that?" You were sitting comfortably on your sofa, reading the latest issue of your favorite magazine *or book* in the dim light when movement across the room caught your attention. It seemed dark and shadowy, but there was nothing there. You returned to your reading—and a moment later, there it was again. You looked up quickly this time and saw the fleeting but distinctly human shape of the shadow pass quickly over the far wall … and disappear.

What was that? Some natural shadow? Your heightened imagination? A ghost? Or was it something that seems to be a spreading phenomenon—apparitions that are coming to be known as shadow people or shadow beings? Perhaps this is an old phenomenon with a new name that is now being discussed more openly, thanks in part to the Internet. Or maybe it's a phenomenon that, for some reason, is manifesting with greater frequency and intensity now than it has in the past.

Those who are experiencing and studying the shadow people phenomenon say that these entities almost always used to be seen out of the corner of the eye and very briefly. But more and more, people are beginning to see them straight on and for longer periods of time. They seem to be a silhouette more times than not. They wear a hat like a fedora and a trench coat, and they carry a cane. Some experiencers testify that they have even seen eyes, usually red, on these shadow beings.

The mysterious sightings have become a hot topic of conversation in paranormal chat rooms and on message boards and websites, and it is being given widespread attention on paranormal talk radio.

What are shadow people, and where do they come from? Several theories have been offered.

The Imagination

The explanation we get from skeptics and mainstream science—usually from people who have never experienced the shadow people phenomenon—is that the phenomenon is nothing more than the active human imagination. It's our minds playing tricks on us; our eyes seeing things for a fraction of a second that aren't really there: illusions, real shadows caused by passing auto headlights, or some similar phenomenon. And without a doubt, these explanations probably can account for some, if not many, experiences. The human eye and mind are easily fooled. But can they account for all cases?

Ghosts

To call these entities ghosts demands first a definition of what we mean by the term "ghost." But by almost any definition, shadow people are somewhat different than ghost phenomena. Whereas ghost apparitions are almost always a misty white color and are vaporous or have a decidedly human form and appearance (very often with discernible clothing), shadow beings are much darker and more shadowlike. In general, although the shadow people often do have a human outline or shape, because they are dark, the details of their appearance are lacking. This is in contrast to many ghost sightings in which the witness can describe the ghost's facial features, style of clothing, and other details. The one detail most often noted in shadow being sightings is their glowing red eyes.

Demons or Other Spirit Entities

The dark countenances and malevolent feelings that are often reported in association with these creatures have led some researchers to speculate that they may be demonic in nature. If they are demons, we have to wonder what their purpose or intent is in letting themselves be seen in this manner. Is it merely to frighten? Some say that they're not demonic at all. If they are demonic in nature, their only purpose in showing themselves in this form is to confuse us. Because they don't want us to know that they're demonic, they will try to fool us, maybe by using a child's voice to trick us into thinking they are children. So is their main job to confuse us and make us fear?

Watchers

We don't know why they're here or why they're watching, but they tend to show up when something bad is going to happen or when there is chaos in an individual's or a family's life (e.g., drug, alcohol, or emotional/physical abuse; some kind of trauma, such as death or a natural disaster). There is no proof that they're the cause of any of these troubles. They just tend to show up and watch during these times. It's also been theorized that our own energies draw them to us.

Astral Bodies

One interesting idea suggests that shadow people are the shadows or essences of people who are having out-of-body experiences. According to Jerry Gross, an author, lecturer, and teacher of astral travel concepts, in his book *We all Travel out of the Body*, we all travel out of the body when we are asleep. Perhaps, this theory says, we are seeing the ephemeral astral bodies of these twilight travelers.

Time Travelers

Another idea states that people from our own future could have found the means to travel to the past—our time. However they are able to accomplish this incredible feat, perhaps in that state they appear to us merely as passing shadows as they observe the events of our timeline.

Interdimensional Beings

Even mainstream science is fairly convinced that there are dimensions other than the one we inhabit. And if these other dimensions exist, who or what (if anything) inhabits them? Some theorists say that these dimensions exist parallel and very close to our own, although invisible to us. And if there are inhabitants in these other dimensions, is it possible that they have found a way to intrude on our dimension and become, at least partially, visible? If so, they could very well appear as shadows.

It has long been held by psychics and other sensitives that beings on other planes of existence are of different "vibrations." Science is beginning to look at reality, on a quantum level, in the same way— that particles of the smallest size exist as vibrations. Perhaps, some theorize, the vibrations of our existence are beginning to mesh with those of another dimension, which accounts for the increase in such phenomena as ghosts, shadow people, and, possibly, aliens.

Aliens

The alien and abduction phenomena are so bizarre that it's no surprise that extraterrestrials are suspects as the shadow people. Abductees have reported in many cases that the gray aliens seem to be able to pass through walls and closed windows, and to appear and disappear abruptly, among more otherworldly talents. Perhaps, too, they can go about their alien agenda disguised in the shadows.

There's a good deal of overlapping among the above ideas, of course. Aliens and ghosts could be interdimensional beings, or aliens could be time travelers—and some believe demons are responsible for all of these disturbing phenomena.

There is no way to prove or disprove any theories about a phenomenon that is so mysterious, that happens so quickly and without warning. Science finds it virtually impossible to catalog or study such phenomena in any methodical way. All we can do, at present, is document personal experiences and try to piece together what the shadow people phenomenon might be. Perhaps it's an old mystery becoming more recognizable, perhaps it represents a doorway to and from different planes of existence—or perhaps it's just shadows.

Chapter Fifteen

ITC, or Instrumental Transcommunication

I t was only a matter of time before researchers began to apply modern technology to the investigation of spirits. Instrumental transcommunication (ITC) uses televisions to capture images from those who have passed away. Users of ITC believe they are capturing evidence from the other side. German ITC researcher Klaus Schreiber gathered images of alleged spirits by aiming a video camera at a television and feeding the output of the video camera back into the TV. The continual loop would often show faces emerging from the mist.

A strange example from Sweden occurred during the burial of Friedrich Juergenson (the Swedish artist and film producer) when an ITC researcher saw an image of a man appear on his TV. He photographed it and discovered after intensive research that it was, in fact, Juergenson. ITC is not limited to television; researchers are now using radios, computers, telephones, and even fax machines. The application of technology is purely to obtain meaningful information, such as voices, images, and text. After a decade of research into the evidence, scientists are finding it hard to simply dismiss this phenomenon.

Perhaps the most controversial device in the paranormal field today is the ghost box (also called Frank's box). It's a device being hailed by some as a "telephone to the dead." The device employs a randomly tuning RF receiver to pull in radio signals, and supposedly, the dead communicate back through it. With a million potential natural sources for the voices, it is impossible to say what they are. The belief seems to be that since spirits manipulate energy in order to manifest and/or move objects, they need some form of energy in order to manifest sound. One of the big problems with the ghost box is that people aren't fully aware of how to use it or how it should even run. The premise of the ghost box is that it scans radio frequencies from one end of the spectrum to the other quickly, picking up random pieces of sound. You're bound to get a number or a single word. Often, though, I've seen people use these boxes as they do a linear sweep, as though it's an EMF meter, going from one station to the very next and so on, and then repeating the process over and over. Unless I'm mistaken, the original setup of Frank's box was supposed to do a *random* sweep of the radio signals while the box was on a table or floor, which would seemingly eliminate the possibility of contamination.

To give you an example of how the ghost box works, let me tell you about what happened to me when using it. During an evidence review at a friend's house, this friend had just bought a new ghost box and asked if I wanted to use it. I said okay and proceeded to open it and put the batteries in it. So it had never been used or manipulated in any way. A new ghost box is built with a phonetic memory, meaning it is programmed with the alphabet. When you start talking to it, it learns words and thus makes it easier for spirits to use it.

After a few minutes of talking to it and it learning its phonetics, it started to talk to me in one or two words at a time. So I started asking it questions, such as "Is there anyone here that would like to talk to me?" I got a response, but it was talking to me in German! What's even more interesting to me is that the ghost box is programmed with the English alphabet. Even though I was speaking to it in English, it was talking back in German. Thank goodness I understand the German language. I started asking in German if there was anyone that wanted to speak to me, and it started telling me *"Vereinigten Paranormal,"* which in English means "united paranormal." It kept telling me that and *"Müssen mit vereinten,"* which means "Must join." The significance of this repeated message is that a couple of weeks before this, I had found an organization on the Internet that deals with the paranormal—a place where you can talk about the paranormal without ridicule or drama. Guess what the name of this great organization is? Yep, that's right. If you remember, I already mentioned it earlier in the book. The organization is United Paranormal International.

At that point I had joined it but hadn't really done anything with them yet. Besides my wife, Crissy, no one else knew about this organization. So for this ghost box—which I had never before used— not only to speak to me, but also to speak to me in German about United Paranormal International, is quite frankly astonishing to me. But if you think this is the end of the story, you're wrong. Flash ahead a couple of months. I was in Virginia City, Nevada, for the St. Mary's ParaCon, and I got a reading from a very well-known and respected medium. During the reading, she asked me if I had been talking with a spirit box or ghost box. I told her that I had. She then asked me if anything strange had happened during the session. I told her it had. She then proceeded to tell me that it was my grandfather, who was fluent in German.

Talk about blowing me away. She then told me that he wanted to tell me to join this organization and that I would become a very important part of this organization. What she didn't know was that I had been with UPI for three months at this point and that I had just been elected as the director of California for the organization. To me, this was the final indication to head in the direction that I am going in today. In fact, my grandfather also came through to tell me to write. This is why I'm writing this book today. This event was my final confirmation to share my experiences and knowledge with the world.

CHAPTER SIXTEEN

Your Basic Investigation

We've gone through all the major pieces of equipment that a paranormal investigator uses on an investigation. So now what do we do with them? As a basic investigator or an experienced one who just wants to have fun, where do we go to investigate? Well, Para cons are a great place to investigate. Popular haunted sites in your local area are great ones too.

Your basic ghost hunt usually doesn't involve a client. These are your everyday, run-of-the-mill, fun investigations that you get to practice your skills on. You can do some research on the place you're going to, but it's not paramount. These types of investigations are also not the types that need to produce the level of scientific data that is required for concrete proof of paranormal activity. However, this does not mean that a piece of evidence that you get at one of these fun investigations can't be used to capture that one crucial piece of evidence that all of us as paranormal investigators are continuously looking for.

As with a client-based investigation, never investigate by yourself. Always have at least one other person with you, if for nothing other than safety. This is paramount to anything you do. Be sure to check the place out during the daytime, as this will help you get a layout of the area. Doing so will allow you to see any hazardous areas that could get you into trouble at night if you don't know they are there. The last thing you want is to get injured during something that was supposed to be a fun outing. Always dress appropriately to the area and the weather. Wear a good supportive pair of shoes with good traction to prevent slipping.

It's up to you regarding what types of equipment you will use during these types of investigations. You should definitely have your pen, paper, flashlight, camera, and voice recorder. Anything more is optional. One other thing you should bring on your investigations that I feel is very important is some kind of *breathing mask*. A lot of the places you will investigate will have dust, asbestos and other potentially harmful contaminants. Always protect yourself. The last thing you need is to get sick while investigating. I also like to bring my EMF reader when I do one of these. You're probably saying that this is a lot of stuff to carry at once. Well, you can buy yourself a vest that has a bunch of pockets in it. I bought two for my wife and I online at the Ghost Hunters website. This allows me to carry all my equipment and keeps my hands free.

When you first arrive at your location, you should walk around the area. Take pictures and, while walking quietly around, try to pick up on any smells, sounds, etc. Take note of the temperature. Work in pairs or small teams. Have one person sweep the area, taking pictures. If using an EMF reader, have the other person do a sweep with it while also taking notes of all the readings that he or she gets at different locations before the investigation begins. You will then have your baseline readings. Later, while the investigation is going on, any type of fluctuation that you get from your baseline readings in that area would warrant further investigation to determine if it is paranormal or not.

Try to thoroughly cover every area or room at the site. If you're doing a residential or office type of space, make sure you don't forget the closets, basements, attics (if you can get access to them), garage, and back and front yards. Also cover patios, porch decks, and swings of any kind. If there are any vehicles, such as an RV or something that belonged to a deceased person who lived there, be sure to check them also. You never know what you might pick up in areas like that.

Now, I know you're having fun investigating, but please always beware of the time. You don't want to get bogged down in one specific area—unless you're getting all kinds of activity; that would warrant some extra time. On average, try not to stay in one place more than forty-five minutes. If a situation warrants extra time, then stay no more than an hour. I've found that when you come back to investigate an area again, you can make that spot or room a priority to investigate further.

Remember during all investigations to be polite and courteous not only to the ghosts but also to property and the people who own the property. When you're finished, please try to return the area to the way it was before your investigation. Please leave quietly and professionally. Remember, you are a representative of not only yourself and your team but also of the paranormal community itself. If you act unprofessionally, it hurts all of us in the field, not just you.

When you return home, you can analyze your photos, EVPs, and all your other evidence. Talk to your team members about what you might have captured. Set up a time and place to get together and discuss all the evidence that was collected by everyone. Make a party out of it—but not a drinking party; you'll want to be sober to be able to look at the evidence closely with clear eyes and ears.

CHAPTER SEVENTEEN

Paranormal Activity Level

B efore I get into how to do an actual investigation for a client, I'd like to provide a guide that will help you determine the level of activity you experience during an investigation. This system was developed by United Paranormal International as a way for all their investigating teams to work under the same guidelines. We call it paranormal activity level, or PAL for short. This system is to be used for the preliminary assignment of activity level / cause based on client reports or preinvestigation interviews. It is also to be used for your post investigation final assignment of activity or cause. Note: The activity level or cause can be changed after investigation results are completed. Please retain all copies of this form and any notes associated to it in the case file for all your cases.

Paranormal Activity Level 1: Personal experiences, such as sounds, touching, or odors. This is the lowest level, and usually this type of activity is nonthreatening. Activity may include sounds of a vague or nebulous nature, such as knocks and bangs; unexplained breezes; light touching; odors; the feeling of being watched; or other nonthreatening activity, such as the recording of typical EVPs.

Paranormal Activity Level 2: Manifestations; elevated physical contact, such as being grabbed, pushed, or scratched; unexplained odors; voices, if witnessed by others; and recorded EVPs of a direct or threatening nature. Activity may include physical objects being moved, such as objects in their normal place later found somewhere else. This is the type of activity that causes the hair on your arms or the back of your neck to stand up. Some even call it the heebie jeebies, for lack of a better term. Seeing what we call shadow people would fall under this category.

Paranormal Activity Level 3: Physical objects moved. Physical contact of an attacking, threatening, violent, or sexual nature.

Paranormal Activity Level 4: Potential signs of preternatural activity, such as levitation, unexplained exhibitions of strength, speaking in tongues, unexplained knowledge—especially of a personal nature about someone (retrocognition) or about future events (precognition)—black or bulging almost sharklike eyes, a lack of blinking for long periods, extreme bodily rigidity, and the inability of several people to lift or move an affected person. These are general indicators of preternatural activity and do not include other indicators, such as certain smells, behavioral changes, or sounds associated with this activity, such as growling or raspy breathing.

Assign a classification of level 4 based on *verified* claims. Reported claims are not verification, and action cannot be taken based solely on client reports. Many investigations may be required to verify claims, so all client reports that fit levels 3 or 4 may require several investigations to verify them.

Special Exception
Level CI: Child(ren) directly affected on any level. This level takes immediate priority over any level other than levels 3 or 4.

Warning! Levels 3 and 4 can be particularly dangerous and are not for the casual or even experienced investigator. It is highly recommended that all investigators leave immediately if levels 3 or 4 are encountered and that a qualified person, such as a demonologist, be brought in for final determination.

Note: Poltergeist activity can appear to exhibit some of the characteristics of many categories and as such can be difficult to identify. It is recommended that a qualified person, such as a parapsychologist, be called in for assistance if poltergeist activity is suspected.

If additional help is needed, then discuss the clients' personal beliefs with them and offer to (1) accompany them to the person of their belief to help eliminate the problem (many times people are not believed, and your presence as a witness will greatly help them get assistance by lending credibility to the claims), (2) try to find someone of their belief to come to their aid, or (3) show video, audio, or other verifiable data to whomever the clients or you choose to provide help.

Investigation Conclusions

(Post your conclusions, actions, and any follow-up investigations required in the comment section of your after-action report.)

Activity classified as
1. Residual
2. Intelligent
3. Poltergeist
4. Preternatural
5. Unknown

Resolution

ICR: Investigation completed and resolved. No further action needed. State how resolved:

1. No activity confirmed.
2. Normal or explainable causes identified.
3. Possible psychological issues suspected.
4. Suspected or confirmed hoax.
5. Activity observed and documented, but no follow-up needed.

ICNF: Investigation completed, activity confirmed, client advised and concurs that no follow-up is necessary. No danger exists to the client.

IC: Investigation completed. Additional investigation needed under original level or reclassified level. State reclassified level in comment section.

CHAPTER EIGHTEEN

Initial Contact

The first thing that you want to do—to me it is the most important thing—is make your initial contact with a new client. That is, send them your questionnaire. This is important, because it will help weed out the "crazies" and the fakers. These are people who just want to see what you do or if you're for real. The questionnaire will weed out these people and leave you with the people who are truly looking for your help. When you have your potential client on the phone, you will want to discuss the purpose of what you do in brief detail. You will also want to send along with your questionnaire the required consent/permission forms and have the client sign them. I will put a copy of the consent/permission forms at the end of the book. After you get the questionnaire back and you've determined that you have a legit client, call the client back and set up your first investigation date.

The following information is what my team uses on its preliminary report. You can tell if your potential client is for real or not. If your potential client does not complete this report or only partially completes it, be wary of the client, as this is a big red flag. I will also put a copy of this form at the end of the book.

- date
- name
- address
- phone number/cell number

- e-mail
- occupant's name, gender, relationship to client, and date of birth

Structural Information
- building type
- bedrooms/bathrooms/square footage/lot size
- additional rooms
- years of occupancy
- known history of location(structural changes, previous occupants, other paranormal activity)
- Have any other buildings been constructed on the site previous to the current one?
- Is there any known history of the surrounding area (old schools, grave sites, old courts, old churches, etc.)?
- Are there any accounts of paranormal activity at your previous residence?
- Are any tragedies or deaths associated with the immediate area or neighborhood? If so, explain.
- Is there any documentation of previous paranormal activity (newspapers, evidence, data, etc.)?

Medical Background
- Any history of alcohol or drug abuse?
- Any history of mental illness?
- Any history of serious trauma (near death, rape, etc.)?
- Please list all medications and prescription items used in the last three years. Include all prescription drugs, over-the-counter drugs, prescription eyeglasses, contact lenses, etc. Please make a separate list for each occupant.
- Have anyone's prescriptions changed recently?
- Any other family history that you think is important for us to know?

Religious History
- What is your religious background?
- When did the current disturbances begin, and what happened at first?

- What did you think of these disturbances?
- Have you looked for ordinary explanations? What makes you think it's paranormal?
- When did the most recent incident occur, and what happened?
- Have the disturbances been increasing in frequency and/or severity since they first began?
- Are events more frequent at certain times of the day, days or the week, or particular months? If so, what times?
- Is there a pattern of any kind to these disturbances that you've noticed (i.e., when the events occurred, what sorts of objects were affected, what locations were involved, who was around at the time, etc.)?
- Is activity more frequent in certain places (for example, in certain rooms of the house) than in others? If so, where?
- Do the occurrences happen more frequently in the presence or vicinity of certain persons than they do with others? If so, state which people. Also, do the events take place when they are not in the area?
- Have there been any witnesses from outside the household? What did they experience, as far as you know?
- If there have been unexplained movements of objects, was there anything strange about the manner in which the objects moved or stopped (e.g., movement around corners, impacts with unusually great force, etc.)?
- Have you or anyone in the residence ever used or experimented with Ouija boards, séances, etc.?
- Have you or anyone in the residence ever used or experimented with the occult (witchcraft, magic, kabbalah) or used any type of occult practices for personal gain (e.g., money, love, revenge, etc.)? If so, please explain.
- How would you like to be helped?
- Have any of the occupants encountered any of the following? (Explain all that apply.)
- voices
- smells/odors
- shadows

- orbs
- smoky forms
- strong random thoughts
- strong feelings/emotions
- cold spots
- hot spots
- recent death of a loved one
- recent anniversary of a loved one's death, birthday, anniversary, etc.
- sounds (walking, running, knocking, etc.)
- door(s) opening/closing
- mood changes, especially in one room
- conversations with spirits
- disappearing objects
- moving objects
- puberty of a family member or emotional stress of adolescents in the area
- renovations to the location
- electrical disturbances (frequent light bulb burnouts, etc.)
- problems with appliances (TVs, radios, stereos, computers, clocks, microwaves, etc.)
- headaches or dizziness
- feelings of being touched
- physical harm (scratches, cuts, bites, etc.)

CHAPTER NINETEEN

Preliminary Interview

N ow that you have arrived at your client's house, you will want to introduce yourselves and have your normal get-to-know-you conversation. This helps you and the client get comfortable with each other. As you're doing this, you can lead into your preliminary interview with your client and any witnesses that might have experienced anything. You should go over anything that stood out on the questionnaire that the client filled out. Prior to conducting the actual interview, the client will need to be thoroughly briefed on what to expect during the investigation and how the process will work, and advised that multiple visits will probably be needed to truly find any answers.

In the past, we've asked many questions to dig into the client's knowledge and understanding of the paranormal. You should ask the client what he or she expects to happen, so that you can get an understanding of what *the client* thinks is going to happen. With the onslaught of TV shows being the main guide for what your client may perceive as how a paranormal investigation should go, the client will need to be thoroughly briefed on what to expect and how the process will work, and this way you can correct the client's view and advise that what he or she has seen on TV is just for entertainment and highly subjective at best. If the client wants the paranormal experiences to stop completely, then this process will obviously be a bit different. Also, the client should be made aware that multiple visits will probably be required to truly find answers. Finally, the client must be aware that he or she will probably have to be involved and participate in parts of the investigation in order for it to work. Let the client know that he or she will not be asked to do anything out of the ordinary and will not be put in harm's way.

After your interview with the client, you should do a walk-through of the place you are investigating. Identify any suspected hot spots where activity has been reported. For example, if your client said that he or she saw a shadowy figure walking through a hallway, you should cover that hallway with one of your static cameras to see if you catch any shadows. If your client told you about a door opening on its own, even after it has been shut all the way, you should cover the door with a camera to see if it will open on its own.

Do a site diagram of how the place is set up so that when you come back to do the actual investigation, you have a plan of attack as to where you want to go first and where you want to set up your equipment. Then figure out where you want to set up your command center. After you have all this done, you are finished with the first stage and you'll just want to set up a second date with your client for the actual investigation.

Note: You want to try to do this preliminary investigation during the week so that you can schedule the actual investigation during the weekend. Usually a Friday or Saturday night is the best time for your full investigation because of everyone's work schedules during the week. Also, since most normal investigations can take up to six to eight hours (that's setup, actual investigation, teardown, and cleanup), you'll need to have that full day off to get your sleep and get back on an even keel before you and your team have to go back to your normal day jobs.

You can also use this time to contact all your team members and let them know that an investigation is coming up that weekend or the next. This will give your team members time to set aside for the investigation. They have lives of their own also, and they might have something already planned on that date. This way everyone will have enough time to schedule—or reschedule, as the case may be—so that all your members can be present.

Also, if you have quite a large team, you will have time to pick who will be present for a given investigation. If you're dealing with a residence, you don't want to have a million people there, overcrowding and possibly contaminating any evidence that you might get. So if someone has made other plans, you can have another member fill that spot. Depending on the size of the dwelling that you're investigating, you may have to choose who can and will be on the investigation. If you do pick who'll be on the different investigations, make sure you rotate the people on each investigation. This way no one gets upset because he or she never gets to go on an investigation. You don't want to lose any members as a result of hurt feelings. In our case, we also go by what each member is trained for. Some of our members aren't trained for dealing with the malevolent side of a house, so they won't be asked to go on those types of investigations. Others aren't trained in cleansing procedures, so they won't be involved in that part.

CHAPTER TWENTY

The Actual Investigation

A true paranormal investigation differs from a basic fun investigation because it involves more equipment than a normal investigation and you have to deal with interviewing clients and doing research at the highest level of investigating. There are many reasons people seek assistance from a paranormal investigator. Some require a specific help that they can't seem to get from their social circle. Some need a sympathetic ear to listen to them, to reassure them that paranormal activity is really happening to them and that they're not going crazy. Unfortunately, we also sometimes have to show them that what they perceive as paranormal activity is not, but that they actually are mentally ill. We then have to send them to a properly trained mental health professional that can help them.

The first and most important thing you should do, at least a couple of days in advance of the actual investigation, is prepare any equipment that will be used for the investigation. The worst thing you can do is get to your client's premises and find out that you forgot a piece of equipment or that you didn't charge something and then have to scramble or do the investigation without an important piece of equipment. Not only does this make you look unprofessional to your client, but it can totally ruin an investigation because then your team will be upset and out of sorts because all they will be able to think of is that they can't use that piece of equipment.

For example, if you forget your voice recorder, your video camera, or—definitely—your flashlights, you could end up missing crucial evidence. So always make sure all of your equipment is charged and ready to go. If certain items use batteries, make sure you've brought plenty of new batteries. I cannot be more emphatic about this; always have plenty of spare batteries on hand. Since it's a known theory that ghosts or spirits can draw their energy from any electromagnetic field in order to talk to you, move an object, or whatever they might do, they will always get that energy from your equipment. Again, this will cause you major problems, not to mention again that it will make you look unprofessional.

You should arrive by 7:00 p.m. This gives you plenty of time to meet with your client again and go over any new occurrences that might have happened since you were there last and set up your equipment. When conducting your actual interviews, you'll want to see what your clients' and witnesses' feelings are about the ghost. You want to get a feeling of what they think is going on and why it's going on. What do they want to happen at the end of the investigation? From here you may delve into the types of events they were engaging in when their experiences happened to them. Just as with your equipment, you want to establish a baseline for how they answer your questions so that you can determine both their physical and mental states.

When beginning your actual interviews, you'll want the environment to be quiet. If you have more than one witness, it's also a good idea to separate them. You'll find that people will open up a lot more when they are not around other family members. This technique will also keep people from feeding information to each other. If at all possible, have at least two team members per witness present while conducting the interviews. This is so one person can concentrate on asking the questions and the other can watch how the witnesses physically act during the Q & A. Most people can use their common sense and tell by watching someone if he or she is lying. Also, one person can write down what the witness is saying.

Most of the time, your witnesses will describe more than one event, so you'll have to break down each event or occurrence individually. You'll want to evaluate any environmental factors, and this may require some reenacting of the specific events to test each theory. If enough evidence points toward a logical explanation, or if the event is just random, then it can be excluded from the "spiritual" part of the investigation if necessary.

This part needs to be very detailed and thorough. If your witness sees a shadow in the hallway, for example, all methods necessary must be used to recreate the exact conditions as they were at the time of the event. You should test the hallway under various conditions. You should see how vehicle headlights, lights in the adjoining rooms, etc., react in the hallway to see if the shadow can be explained. If all logical scenarios have been thoroughly investigated and the event is still not explained, then the spiritual part of the investigation should be conducted to explain what is going on.

There are a couple of ways to do this. One is to start with asking the witnesses what they were doing before the event occurred. Have them describe themselves and their environment before the event in as much detail as possible. This should help with two things. First, it will help them remember more detail about what took place. Second, it will give you a possible clue or clues as to possible paranormal triggers or a possible logical explanation regarding the event.

Make sure that you get the client to report everything, even if he or she thinks it's not important to the case. As the client or witness is telling the story, be sure to encourage him or her by asking questions. Ask for specific information about the setting during their story. Ask about the location and the environment (was it sunny, raining, windy, day, night, etc.?). If the witness has pets, where were they during the event? Were the lights on or off? Did the witness notice anything happening around him or her? Make sure you get specifics about the witness's feelings during all of this. You can ask questions like "How do you feel about what you're describing?" This helps to pull out more detail through the witness's remembering.

When the witness has finally completed a story, tell the witness you want him or her to tell the story again, starting from different parts of the story. This is not to just find out if your client is lying (because when you break up the story into different parts, it's harder for someone who is lying to keep the story straight) but also to go deeper into it. This will allow the witness to really begin to remember the finer details about the event. Again, if all logical scenarios have been thoroughly investigated and not everything has been explained, then it's time for the spiritual or ghostly part of the investigation to proceed.

Now that you've moved on to the ghost part of the investigation, you'll want to set up any equipment that you will be using. This is when you want to refer back to your initial interview and your diagram that you made of the premises, so that you can remember where your hotspots are and set up your camera equipment, and anything else that you need to set up, in the proper spaces so that you maximize your coverage area. Like I said before, mark all of your hotspots with colored tape so that you remember where they are. Once your equipment is set up, you should have a meeting with all your members to set up your procedures on how the investigation is going to be run.

You should assign every member a task so that there is no communication mix-up on what responsibilities each person has. Have someone to watch your DVR screen to look for any occurrence in any room that you're monitoring and be the control officer. This person can see where everyone is, and in case of an emergency, he or she can be the one with a cell phone that can call the authorities if needed. You'll want to set up mini teams and assign them to starting points. Then, within those teams, you'll want to know who's taking pictures, who's taking the EMF readings, who's making the EVP recordings, etc. This way nothing is forgotten and everyone is responsible for some part of the process. Once everyone knows and understands what each and every person's role is for the investigation, you can start your investigation. You should be ready to do this no later than 9:00 p.m.

While your team lead and whoever else you have doing your interviews are busy, this is the perfect moment to have your mediums do their walkthrough. You will want to let your medium or mediums, empaths, etc., do their walkthrough and give you their impressions of what they feel. Remember, your medium is not a means to know all; he or she is just another tool in your arsenal that can help validate any evidence that you get.

I know I'm going to get a lot of grief from those out there that don't like using mediums, empaths, or anyone of the sort. They claim that their use is not scientific. But I'll tell you right now that if you're not using mediums or empaths as part of your investigative arsenal, you're wasting a great resource. I've been on too many investigations using our mediums in which they said they felt or saw something and, when we stopped to take pictures and record EVPs, we've gotten some of our best evidence. To give you an example, on one of our investigations one of our sensitives said she had a feeling of being touched on her shoulder. I immediately started taking pictures around her, and we did an EVP session. Not only did we catch a big blue orb over the shoulder that she felt being touched, but we also got a "Hello" on our EVP recording a couple of seconds after that. That was three different points of evidence that corresponded with each other. To me, that indicated there was probably a spirit or entity there at that moment. So I would encourage teams to use mediums and empaths to give added strength, rather than shy away from them.

You should take a break after about forty-five minutes to take a breather. Get all teams back together at this time and discuss what happened during your investigation. When you start up again, switch areas, and if either team or both got any type of activity, such as an EVP, the other team should try to repeat what the previous team did to see if they get the same results. This will help to validate your evidence. Continue to do this until you have covered the entire premises. By 3:00 a.m., you should be done with your investigation and start tearing down your equipment and packing it up and storing it away. Make sure that the client knows that you're done, and have the client do a walkthrough with you to make sure that everything is cleaned up and satisfactory to him or her. Another team member can join you both on the walk through if necessary. Once the client is happy with the premises, then go home for some well-deserved sleep.

CHAPTER TWENTY-ONE

Using a Medium

O kay, so you want to incorporate a psychic/medium into your investigations. Before we get into how to find one, let's go over some misconceptions of what psychics are and what they are not. Psychics are often thought of as people with supernatural powers. Much worse, it is oftentimes thought by other people that their powers come from the darkness. Sometimes people who believe in psychics believe for the wrong reasons. Thinking that psychics can perform extraordinary wonders as though they are magicians is a misconception that has hampered psychics' actual purpose and usefulness for eons.

Some people think that psychics can read their minds and know what everyone is thinking all the time. They assume that psychics can tell how many fingers one is holding up behind his or her back. This is just not true. Psychics are just ordinary people like you and me. They just have extraordinary powers that God or the universe has given them. All psychics have the gift of empathy. This gift allows psychics to receive psychic readings that tell them if one is happy, sad, depressed, or lonely. Furthermore, their clairvoyance can allow them to dig deeper and understand why a person is feeling such a way. Psychics can also gain access to a person's spirit guides through psychic readings. The guides can tell a lot about a person.

Another misconception that some people have about dealing with psychics is the belief that psychics are fortune tellers and can predict the future. Psychics cannot tell the future, for the main reason that the future is not definite or absolute; it is not written in stone. So how come psychics can tell what's going to happen? This is possible because when a psychic tunes into a person's or animal's energy and spirit guides, that psychic can only give advice on what he or she sees; the psychic cannot make anyone take that path. Free will is the key to everyone's life.

People have always been afraid of curses, and some of them believe these can come from psychics. The real score here is that this is entirely not true. Curses are wishes for someone's fall or demise, which is what a witch does. Since the beginning of time, people have confused witches with psychics. Witches create curses, which in some people's minds are either real or not—the trick is whether the person believes or not. Curses are, when you get right down to it, just wishes. However, these wishes will never come true, no matter how much a person might want to believe in them. Whether witches of the old had any real power or not, those spells—or whatever you want to call them—have been either lost or destroyed long ago.

Psychics are not psychic all the time. When people say that nothing bad will ever happen to psychics because they know what is going to happen before it happens is total hogwash. When psychics do a psychic reading, they tune into a person's guides to tell them what is happening to that person and what might happen to them next. Again, the future is not a constant. For it to be a constant would mean that nothing could change. The person could make one decision only, and so the future could be told. This is not true; a person changes his or her mind constantly, changing decisions that he or she is going to make, so a psychic can only see what *could* happen. But when that person leaves and the session has ended, then the psychic will stop tuning into that person's energy. After that point, anything can happen. The same is true of psychics themselves. They do not listen to their guides all the time; otherwise, they would go nuts. It is our free will that we as humans have to change our minds that makes the future a total unknown and unable to predict.

When you sit back and think about it, psychics are really just cold readers. Cold reading is the process of discerning different types of information and other interesting facts about a person using his or her body language. This information can very well apply to any person on the planet. However, not all cold readings can be accurate and work perfectly for a certain person. Although there are people out there who do cold readings and claim to be psychics, real psychics need to get in tune with their clients' spirit guides to be successful.

There is another misconception out there also, and that is that psychics are mediums. A good place to start, perhaps, is in reminding ourselves of the difference between psychics and mediums. In my perception, a psychic is someone who communicates with the spirits of the dead and with spirit guides or other entities—such as angels, for example. A medium, on the other hand, typically picks up on information through a series of visions seen through what they like to call their third eye or mind's eye. Other senses may also be stimulated, such as their sense of taste, hearing, sight, or smell. There is also the physical sense of temperature change. Each medium is different and may use just one or any combination of these senses when picking up information. Some, like the well-known Scott Russell Hill in Australia and Alison Dubois of the TV show *Medium*, do it in their sleep. Many psychics also possess some sort of mediumistic ability and use the two in combination. I actually use these types on my paranormal teams.

Empaths are another group of gifted people who share close connections with those who are psychic, in that they often experience the emotions of others. That is the key difference between someone feeling empathy with someone and someone having sympathy for them. Understanding the suffering of another is not the same as experiencing their suffering with them.

Types of mediums can be broken down into different groups, such as trance or channeling mediums, physical mediums, sketch medium, and automatic writing mediums.

A channeling medium is a person who channels a spirit into himself or herself to help that spirit communicate through him or her. A physical medium lets a spirit use his or her body to communicate; however, this is almost never used, because mediums don't like losing total control of their body. If someone comes to you and wants to use this method, he or she is probably a scam artist out to use you.

A sketch medium uses a sketch pad and pencil to draw pictures to help spirits communicate.

An automatic writing medium will let his or her guides write down whatever communication the other side needs to get across to the person whom the medium is dealing with.

Psychics, like mediums, can be broken into different groups. A clairvoyant is usually someone who sees things, either with his or her physical eyes or third eye. Most people use the term "clairsentient," as these people sense things rather than actually see them, but the movies you see inside your mind could also be considered a type of sight (e.g., second sight), so perhaps the distinction is not important.

Clairaudients are people who actually hear voices externally, rather than inside their minds.

Clairalients are people who use their sense of smell to detect odors that don't have any kind of physical source. Instances of this could include smelling the perfume or the cigarette smoke of a deceased relative, used as a sign of their presence around us. When our sense of smell is strong and distinct, we may find that certain smells connect us to past memories, or we may be drawn to working as a florist, a wine taster, or a perfume fragrance creator.

Clairgustince is the ability to taste something that isn't actually there. This experience oftentimes comes from out of the blue when a deceased loved one is attempting to communicate a memory or association we have with a particular food or beverage that reminds us of them.

Claircognizance is the ability of clear knowing. This refers to instances when we have knowledge of people or events that we would not normally have knowledge about. For those of us with claircognizance, spirits imprint us with truths that simply pop into our minds from out of nowhere. An example of this would be a premonition: a forewarning of something that will happen in the future. Claircognizance requires tremendous faith because there's often no practical explanation for why we suddenly "know" something. Many philosophers, professors, doctors, scientists, religious and spiritual leaders, and powerful sales and business leaders tend to be highly intuitive and seem to just know the facts with a sense of certainty. If this is you, consider claircognizance one of your dominant senses.

As you can see, the term "psychic" is more than a catch-all term that is overused to cover a multitude of abilities that vary in so many ways that it's not fair to the people who use these abilities on a daily basis. I hope after reading this chapter, people can realize that being a psychic or medium is not all hoodoo and voodoo. Psychics and mediums are people just like us, not some all-knowing beings from another planet. So the next time you're walking down the street or eating at your favorite eatery and you say hello to the nice man or woman who is walking by or sitting next to you and, during your normal conversation with that person, you learn that he or she is a medium or something else, please don't just think that the person is a psychic—or worse, weird. Mediums and psychics are just like you and me.

So how do you find one? If you are searching for a genuine psychic/medium to assist you in your investigations, don't be too hasty in your selection. Here are some tips that should help you in finding the real deal. One of the ways to try to find a local medium/psychic is to first see if you have a metaphysical store or some kind of center that deals in metaphysical workshops. Here in Fresno, my wife and her Lightworkers Foundation group use a tai chi center to have monthly meet-ups for their psychics and mediums to work on their craft. I guarantee that at least one or two would be willing to help you out with your investigations. This helps them use their talents in an actual application setting. This not only helps you in your investigations, but it helps them become more proficient also. I guarantee that they would love to get involved in paranormal investigations.

CHAPTER TWENTY-TWO

Historical Site Research

Okay, some of you out there are saying, "Why are you introducing your research section now? Shouldn't it be done before the investigation?" Well, here is again where the fun investigation is different from the private investigation. I believe you can do research on a historical place before the actual investigation because you're just having fun and you're not trying to use any of the evidence to prove anything. Knowing beforehand can help you plan the investigation. You don't have to waste time and energy figuring out where the hot spots are.

When it comes to a private investigation, in my opinion, you want to do your research after your investigation because you don't want any tainted evidence. Take EVPs, for example. If you have a name or some knowledge of a place or event, it's already in your head. You might hear a name such as Ted on a recording, but because the owner told you about someone named Ken, you're going to already be attuned to hearing "Ken" though the name is really Ted. This is going to taint your whole investigation, which is not going to help you or your client. Trust me; I've seen this happen before. You don't want to have any precognitive suggestions in your head.

So with this having been said, an important part of the paranormal investigation process is research. This includes property history, city history, environmental concerns, geological and man-made data, and demographic information. We investigate all possible causes of activity that seem paranormal, as well as learn about the people who lived on the property in the past. There are many aspects to consider when something unexplained is going on, and you should try to leave no stone unturned in helping a client find answers.

When researching property history, the best place to start is the county records building. These records are kept in the county seat, which is the city or town in a county that has the courthouse and county government offices. Some records are available online, but it is best to go to the county recorder or tax assessor to request the information. The public library is also an excellent resource for city directories and US census records. These records can trace a property back to the year it was purchased, along with the names of the residents. From there, the names can be researched in obituaries, birth and marriage records, and newspaper archives to further put together the history of the property and the people who lived in the home or on the land.

Another aspect of investigating paranormal claims is looking for any environmental concerns or superfund sites in the area. A superfund site is an area where toxic waste has been disposed of and is designated for cleanup by the Environmental Protection Agency (EPA). If there are known neurotoxins present in your area, they will be documented. There are levels of neurotoxins that may affect people to the point at which they believe that what they are experiencing is paranormal. Carbon monoxide levels also need to be tested, as well as any mold or toxins in the home. This is not only to rule out potential paranormal activity, but also as a safety measure. The EPA website is constantly updating information for superfund sites all across the country.

Geological data for the area should also be examined and documented. Research the geological surveys of a property or surrounding area to discover what minerals are present as well as the content of the soil. This data should be collected to get a better understanding of what geological factors might contribute to activity. Local libraries have much of this information, as well as the US Geological Surveys (USGS) website.

You should also document anything man-made in the area that might affect equipment or possibly be a cause for activity. Examples of such things are power lines, communication towers, and nearby radio stations, especially anything within a two-mile radius of the property. Nearby power lines can cause high EMF readings, and towers transmit signals that might get picked up on audio equipment.

The history and demographics of the entire city or area in which the property is located should also be researched. You should document such things as landmarks, cemeteries, parks and forest preserves (which were often Native American campgrounds or hunting grounds at one time), religions and nationalities of the area, and anything else significant. Any connection that the area may have had to wars or skirmishes that occurred should also be documented, as well as accidents and weather catastrophes that may have caused a lot of unexpected deaths. Much of this information can be found through a city's historical society and local library. All of this is done to assist in helping you and the client find some answers as to what is being experienced. Note: None of the research should be done without express written permission from the client to access any records for the property. Additionally, no personal information for any client should be revealed to anyone, *ever*, unless authorized by the client. All of the research information we gather is added to our client database. The database is used to cross-reference key elements found during the research to see if any correlations are found. Clients provide a wonderful opportunity to research and learn about what causes activity that seems to be unexplained.

Gathering all possible data and examining the history of the home and area are part of what may one day help find those explanations. I hope that the information that I've given you here can help you do some solid research that will show your client that you are truly a professional and not an amateur.

CHAPTER TWENTY-THREE

The Evidence Review

N ow comes the most boring, yet most exciting, part of the investigation process. Your investigation is now over, and you have all kinds of evidence that you've collected. Now you need to analyze your data from all the video and audio tapes that you've made. This takes a lot of long, boring hours; however, if you can authenticate one or two anomalous pieces of your evidence, then it's all worth it. How do you go about doing this?

It doesn't matter what evidence you start with, but I'll start with the video. There are quite a few places to go to look at your video. One of the places I like to go to is videolan.org. This application allows you to view video, loop video, jump to a specific video time, and speed up or slow down the video. You can look at audio and video at the same time, as long as it's part of the same file. The only downside is that VLC does not allow you to crop out video frames. This means that if you only want to see a particular ten-second clip, you will need to use another application to extract that clip from the original film.

For photos we use Photo ME. It's an application that allows us to get to the exchangeable image file format (Exif) data for a digital image (picture). Exif data is embedded within the image file itself and contains information about the image, such as the following: date taken, date modified, type of camera used, ISO setting, f-number, flash usage, aperture setting, etc. This information assists us during a review of the image for many reasons. The primary reason is that it tells us if an image has been modified since it was taken. Another key reason is that some camera models have known defects with the camera and/or firmware for the camera that will cause a false positive (something that looks paranormal but is not) to appear on the image. Information such as flash usage, f-number, aperture, etc. helps us determine if the setting used when taking the image caused a false positive.

Photoscape is an online application that allows you to edit your photos. However, we use it to apply different filters to the photos to get a closer look at what is there. We will review it in black-and-white, with heat signatures applied, etc.

Besides these applications, there are many, many more than can be used. Each application has its own use and features that can be useful. No matter what application is used, just remember that most of what is captured in an image can be explained and is more than likely not paranormal. However, if you do get lucky enough to take a photo that falls into that 1 percent, pass it our way.

During an investigation, we put out digital recorders to capture audio data in order to capture an EVP, electronic noise phenomenon (ENP), or a disembodied voice during the investigation. When we review the audio data, we use a PC loaded with an audio software application. There are many, many applications available for use. Some are free, and some need to be purchased. As a team, we chose to use an application called Audacity (see photo below). This application allows us to highlight parts of the audio file, loop it, magnify it, etc. We use Audacity because it is free, easy to use, allows for looping, and exports data clips easily in MP3 or WAV format. Here is a link to the Audacity software site: http:// audacity.sourceforge.net/.

A software application will also allow you to determine the frequency that the EVP/ENP occurred in. The primary reason this is important is that it permits you to track patterns and assist with proving theories. There is a theory in the paranormal field that EVPs aren't heard (making it a disembodied voice) because they occur in a frequency range that cannot be heard by human ears. By using such an application, you can track that information and watch for patterns.

One of the best applications for frequency identification is Adobe

Audition. Adobe Audition must be purchased, but it does have features that other applications do not. The most important is its ability to use it to extract audio from a video file. We use this feature quite a bit. No matter which application you use, there are two things to remember: (1) each team member should use the same application, and (2) a true EVP, ENP, or disembodied voice should be able to be played in its original state and not modified in any way.

CHAPTER TWENTY-FOUR

A Client's Point of View

W hat if you're a person who is having experiences or needs help? Where do you go to choose a team? Whom do you talk to in order to find one? Let's look at how to identify the type of team you are searching for. This is especially vital if you are suffering from a hostile haunting:

1) What is their mission statement? What do they stand for?

2) How much experience do they have, and what does that experience consist of? Watching television and reading books are not considered experience. While there is no such thing as a certified investigator, most teams get some kind of training from somewhere; find out whether the team you are examining has any.

3) Look at the team itself and each investigator. What are their paying professions and educational backgrounds? Read their bios if possible. All of these items should be on the team's website if they are legitimate. Make sure they are not letting just anyone onto their team.

4) Does the group have a formal set of investigation guidelines and rules? Do they require each investigator to attend seminars and other forms of training? Do they have liability disclosures and client contracts? This can indicate how serious and professional the team is.

5) Are they only going to public investigations or holding meet-up groups? Note: Any group that is willing to accept anyone wanting to explore the paranormal as a team member without requiring some kind of training is not a real team. Such groups are only meet-ups—groups of people out for the thrill of it (unless they are run by a verified paranormal team or psychic). Stay away from teams that are mostly teenagers or young adults; the necessary maturity level is just not there. There should be some mature adults leading the team.

6) One major problem in this field is *self-titling.* Anyone can earn the title "reverend" or "minister" by purchasing it through the Internet. The term "authentic" means that someone has theological training through either a college or a church, or at least a certified or accredited school. (Most people who hold self-titles on Facebook are not authentic.) These people can actually make the problem worse than better, so be careful. Note that the newest addition to these self-titles is the term "demonologist." True demonologists have spent many years in a formal educational system, studying theology and the occult; or they have studied for years under a church-trained demonologist.

7) Do they charge for their services? Never pay any team to come out to investigate or perform a cleansing. This is a major red flag, as no one can ever guarantee to rid your home of spirits.

8) Guaranteed services: Again, no one can ever promise to rid your home of spirits. Also remember that not all spirits need to be removed; only small percentages are considered hostile, and most are misunderstood because of television programs creating fear and terror.

9) Get references if they are available. If not, you can also Google the team to see what others are saying about them and to perform a background check.

10) Examine their website with a fine-toothed comb. Especially pay attention to their evidence if they have it available. If they have clips or videos of them investigating, are they using provocation? Are they

disclosing private information? There are many teams out there that are happy to post a picture of your home all over the Internet without ever thinking of privacy.

11) What methods do they follow? Are they 100 percent science-based, or are they spiritual? If yours is a private case, it is best to use a team with a mixture of scientific and spiritual aspects. That is how my team works. Also make sure the group is not 100 percent male or 100 percent female. There should be an equal balance.

12) Watch out for any teams or persons asking for travel expenses to come and investigate, especially if you're local. This is a huge red flag that they are not out to help you, but themselves.

Lastly, it is up to the client looking for help or the person wanting to join a paranormal team to make sure the team is reputable. There are no governing authorities over the paranormal field, which makes it even more important to do your research beforehand. With so many new paranormal-themed shows coming out, a sideshow of thrill seekers has been created. Be careful and educate yourself before ever becoming involved with any team. Always remember that the television shows are only entertainment and there is a lot of exaggeration and staging involved with them; they are only out for ratings and not to educate the public. I believe there will eventually be some sort of governing body over the paranormal field, but until then it is essential to do your research and not buy into the television hype!

Chapter Twenty-Five

Closing Remarks

As I said before, paranormal investigation is the research of events or phenomena that science can't or won't explain. Sometimes this means investigating a suspected haunting. Other times paranormal investigation means looking into what is causing people to report sightings of a strange creature or shadow. In other cases, you'll be chasing down certain sounds that people report hearing. No matter what the case might be, paranormal investigation, in my mind, is rarely a boring field.

The field of paranormal investigation, first and foremost, requires one to possess a rational mind, a calm disposition, and, most importantly (in my opinion), a set of very calm nerves. Often, things that seem paranormal at first turn out to be nothing and have perfectly natural explanations. Therefore, while it is important to keep an open mind, it's even more important not to go rushing to conclusions and conjectures without the proper evidence—especially if you want to be taken seriously as a paranormal investigator. The ghost hunter can get away with it, but an investigator cannot. Those who are quick to draw conclusions are often not cut out to be paranormal investigators.

With all this having been said, you now possess, I hope, the valuable knowledge that only a select few ever get. I hope it will help you make the right decisions when you're out on your next investigation. I've tried to be as honest and forthright as I can with all of you. The opinions expressed herein are based on my personal firsthand experiences and those of other investigators that I hold in high esteem for their experience and knowledge. Your experiences and opinions may differ. However, if we are to be taken seriously by mainstream science, we need to work together to make what we do in the field universal so that we can finally become a mainstream science that is regulated and certified. By following the methods and procedures I have talked about in this book, we can finally do just that.

Resources

Paranormal Societies
For those interested in furthering their paranormal investigation or research, here's a list of teams and organizations that can help develop your techniques. These are, in my opinion, some of the best teams out there right now. I have provided locations, contact info, and websites so that you can check them out and contact them if necessary.

ALABAMA
   Alabama Paranormal Exploration Society
   www.alabama-paranormal-exploration-society.com Contact: Christy or Jason

ALASKA
   Alaska Ghost Hunting
   www.alaskaghosthunting.com Contact: John Francis (907) 223-0371

ARIZONA
   Border Paranormal
   www.borderparanormal.7p.com

   Chandler Paranormal Research
   www.chandlerparanormal.ning.com Contact: Bruce Rice

ARKANSAS

After Midnight Paranormal Investigations
www.aftermidnightparanormalinvestigationteam.com
Contact: Russ Keeler

CALIFORNIA

11th Hour Paranormal Research Society
www.11thhourparanormal.com Contact: Crissy Campbell or
Chad Stambaugh (559) 704-8266 or 355-3522

California Society for Paranormal Assistance Research
www.cspar.org Contact: John Fowler

Alameda Paranormal
www.alamedaparanormal.com Contact: Sommer

X Paranormal
www.xparanormal.org Contact: Cory Caplinger

COLORADO

American Association of Paranormal Investigators
www.ghostpi.com Contact: Stephen Weidner (702) 432-
2746

CONNECTICUT

Connecticut Ghost Chasers
www.ctghostchasers.com Contact: David Teer

Connecticut Ghost Investigations
www.connecticutghostinvestigations.com Contact: Jeff
Banks

DELAWARE

Delaware Ghost Hunters
www.delawareghosthunters.com Contact: Carl or Gina

FLORIDA

Paranormal Extreme
www.paranormalextreme.com Contact: Paul Benstine (239) 677-8973

Fire and ICE Paranormal Investigators of Florida
www.fireandiceparanormal.com Contact: Gary "Ice" Walters and Virginia "Red" Walters (239) 247-5578

Florida Paranormal Spirit Activity Investigations
www.diannespirilight.com Contact: Dianne

GEORGIA

Past Life Investigations
www.pastlifeinvestigation.net Contact: Debra or Michael Shigetoni

HAWAII

Hawaiian Island Ghost Hunters
www.hawaiinislandghosthunters.com (885) NO-GHOST Contact: Preston Galera

IDAHO

Paranormal Idaho
www.paranormalidaho.com (208) 573-4871 Contact: Jamie Sorenson

ILLINOIS

TnT Paranormal Investigations
www.tntparanormal.com Contact: Melissa Tanner

Bump in the Night Paranormal
www.bumpinthenightparanormal.com Contact: Lori Taylor-Esposito

INDIANA

ALAB Paranormal
www.alabparanormal.com Contact: Craig

Columbus Ghost Trackers of Indiana
www.columbusghosttrackers.com Contact: Deb

IOWA
Calhoun County Paranormal Investigators
www.calhouncountypi.com Contact: Seth Alne

Paranormal Investigation Truth Seekers
www.p-i-t-s.webs.com Contact: Rob Ridgeway

KANSAS
Kansas Paranormal Investigations
www.kansasparanormalinvestigators.com Contact: Vicky
Wichita Paranormal
www.wichitaparanormal.com Contact: Shane Elliott

KENTUCKY
Campbell County Paranormal Research
www.campbellcountyparanormalresearch.com   Contact:
Brad Johnson

DTR Paranormal
www.dtrparanormal.webs.com Contact: David or Tasha

LOUISIANA
Bayou Paranormal
www.bayouparanormal.net Contact: Starr

Carpe Nocturne Paranormal Society
www.carpenocturneparanormalsociety.weebly.com Contact:
Christine Watkins

Ghost N Specters Paranormal Investigations & Research
www.ghostnspecters.info Contact: Tammy

MAINE
Central Maine Paranormal Investigations
www.maineghostseekers.com Contact: Stacey Farrington

Coastal Maine Paranormal Society
www.coastalmaineparanormalsociety.com Contact: Kim
Kennebec County Paranormal Society
www.kennebecparanormal.org (207) 314-7857 Contact:
Dan

MARYLAND
Another Dimension Paranormal Team
www.anotherdimensionparanormalteam.webs.com Contact:
Laura

Antietam Paranormal Society
www.antietamparanormalsociety.com Contact: Rebecca or
Jeremy Boyer

MASSACHUSETTS
C.A.S.E. Paranormal
www.caseparanormal.com Contact: Charles Foley

Para Boston Investigators
www.para-boston.com Contact: Scott

MICHIGAN
Bay Area Supernatural Encounters
www.bayarease.com Contact: Kris

BPI Paranormal Investigations
www.bpiparanormalinvestigators.org   Contact: Erika
Benson

Paranormal Research and Investigative Society of Michigan
www.prisomparanormal.wix.com Contact: Tom Vlassis

MINNESOTA
Afterlife Paranormal Study Group
www.alparanormal.com Contact: Jason Navotne

Central Minnesota Ghost Hunters
www.centralmnghosthunters.com Contact: Amie (763) 442-4495

MISSISSIPPI
Central Mississippi Supernatural Investigations
www.mississippiparanormalinvestigations.webs.com Contact: Wil Bane (662) 705-0644

Haunted Mississippi Paranormal Research
www.hauntedmississppi.com Contact: Marc Brunson

MISSOURI
60th Street Paranormal
www.60thstreetparanormal.webs.com Contact: Kira or Heather

Clay County Paranormal Research Society
www.claycountypara.org Contact: Debbie

Elite Paranormal of Kansas City
www.eliteparanormalkc.com Contact: Rob Garcia

MONTANA
Montana Association of Paranormal Studies
www.montanaparanormal.org Contact: Case Manager (406) 216-2940

Montana Paranormal Research Society
www.mtprs.org Contact: Dustin Benner

NEBRASKA
Crossroads Para-Investigation
www.cpinebraska.com Contact: Ted Pool

Duncan Paranormal Society
www.duncanparanormalsociety.webs.com Contact: Brian or Amber (505) 918-6221

NEVADA
Elite Vegas Paranormal Society
www.elitevegasparanormalsociety.com Contact: Brian .or Linda Purdy

G.A.T. Investigations
www.gatnv.com Contact: Kymberli or Joe

NEW HAMPSHIRE
Central New Hampshire Paranormal Society
www.centalnhps.com Contact: Eric Perry

North East Paranormal Associates
www.nepanh.com Contact: Mark Raiche

NEW JERSEY
D2 Paranormal
www.d2paranormal.com Contact: Debbie Manocchio (609) 502-1227

Paranormal Consulting & Investigations
www.pcinj.org Contact: Joanne Emmons or Pat Kibby

NEW MEXICO
Central New Mexico Ghost Investigations
www.cnmgi.com Contact: Virginia

Purple Sage Paranormal
www.purplesageparanormal.com Contact: Roger Barton

NEW YORK
Albany Paranormal Research Society
www.paranormalalbany.com Contact: Debbie Stockwell

B.A.R.S. Paranormal
www.barsparanormalgroup.com Contact: Sherri Grin

NORTH CAROLINA
Carolina Anomaly Spirits & Paranormal Researchers
www.caspr.tk Contact: Wanda Stone

Time Stoppers Paranormal
www.timestoppersparanormal.org Contact: Heather Garner

NORTH DAKOTA
Midstate Paranormal Research Society
www.midstateparanormal.webs.com Contact: Matt Hagen
Night Light Paranormal Investigations
www.nlpiofgrandforks.com

OHIO
A New Day Paranormal
www.anewdayparanormal.weebly.com Contact: Sue

Celestial Spirit Investigators
www.celestialspiritinvestigators.org Contact: Jeanine

OKLAHOMA

PENNSYLVANIA
All 4 Paranormal
www.all4paranormal.com Contact: Lee or Harry

Complete Paranormal Services
www.epsparanormal.com Contact: Keith

Sisters of Ghost Hunting
www.sisterofghosthunting.com Contact: Pam Waldo (215) 441-0530

RHODE ISLAND
Black Cross Paranormal
www.blackcrossparanormal.com Contact: Stephen or Ryleigh Black

Spirit Finders Paranormal Investigators
www.spirit-finders.com Contact: Chris Andrews

SOUTH CAROLINA
Athena Research Group
www.orioninvestigators.webs.com Contact: EJ Lukas (843) 424-8053

Phasma Paranormal
www.phasmaparanormal.com Contact: Case Manager

SOUTH DAKOTA
Black Hills Paranormal Investigations
www.bhparanormal.com Contact: Mark Rowland or Maurice Miller

S.A.N.D. P.I.T. South & North Dakota Paranormal Investigative Team
www.sandpit.webs.com Contact: Joanie

TENNESSEE
Afterlife Research and Consulting
www.afterliferesearchandconsulting.com Contact: Rick Tatum

Cryptic Shadows Paranormal Research
www.csparanormalresearch.com Contact: Angela Ashton

TEXAS
Austin Paranormal Group
www.austinparanormal.com Contact: Amanda Foster

Brownwood Paranormal Society
www.brownwoodparanormalsociety.com Contact: John or Joy Dillard

UTAH

4-Element Paranormal
www.4-element-paranormal.com Contact: Tim or Lindsay

Mountain West Paranormal
www.mwparanormal.com Contact: Nathan Tooley

VERMONT

Green Mountain Paranormal Society
www.gmparanormal.wordpress.com Contact: Jennifer Perellie

Hometown Paranormal
www.honetownparanormalvt.com Contact: Rev. Michael Manning

VIRGINIA

3:33 a.m. Paranormal Research
www.333amparanormalresearch.com Contact: Krystal Porras
(703) 586-0158

Eastern States Paranormal
www.easternstatesparanormal.com Contact: Roy

WASHINGTON

Aghost Investigations
www.aghost.org Contact: Ross Allison

Apart Paranormal
www.apartofwa.com Contact: David (253) 666-3555

WEST VIRGINIA

Afterlife Paranormal Investigations
www.afterlifeparanormal5.webnode.com Contact: Jason or
Mona Boyd

Appalachian Paranormal Center
www.appalachianparanormalcenter.com Contact: Matt
Shanblin

WISCONSIN

S.O.S. Investigations

www.sosinvestigated.weebly.com Contact: Cory Jandrin

Shadows of Light

www.shadowsoflightpg.webs.com Contact: Rob

Tri-County Paranormal Group

www.tricountyparanormalgroup.com Contact: Brandon Schilling

WYOMING

Paranormal Research Society of Casper

www.paranormalresearchsocietyofcasper.org Contact: Lisa

Every single one of these groups is reputable, and none of them charge for their services—that should be the top priority on anyone's list of which team to use. There are many more groups and organizations out there; however, for various reasons, I will not endorse them, and therefore, they will not be on my list.

I'd also like to add these two websites for people who wish to have a place to buy their equipment at a very reasonable price:

- www.ghosthunterstore.com
- www.ghoststop.com

These two companies are very friendly and will answer any questions that you may have. Every piece of equipment that my team uses has been bought from one of these two great websites. I'd also like you to check out United Paranormal International. Their web address is www.unitedparanormalinternational.ning.com.

FORMS

The following pages are some forms that we use in our investigations and that you, my readers, may copy freely to use in your team's investigations.

PRELIMINARY CASE REPORT
PARANORMAL CONSULTATION

Date:

Name

Address:

City: State: Zip Code:

Phone Number: Cell Number:

Email:

Occupants' Names Including Yourself	Gender	Relationship	Date / time of Birth (mm/dd/yy)

Structural Information

Building Type (Detached Residence, Duplex, Condo, Apartment, Commercial, etc.): _____

Bedrooms [   ]   Bathrooms [   ]   Square Feet: [   ]   Lot Size (Sq. Feet): [   ]

Additional Rooms & Other Information:

How many years and/or months have occupants lived at the location?

Any known history of location? (Structural changes, previous occupants, other paranormal activity, etc.)

Have any other buildings been constructed on the site previous to the current one? If so explain:

Is there any known history of the surrounding area? (Ex: Old schools, grave sites, old courts, old churches, etc.)

Are there any accounts of paranormal activity at your previous residence?

Were any tragedies or deaths associated with the immediate area or neighborhood? If so, explain:

Is there any documentation of previous paranormal activity? (Ex: Newspaper clippings, evidence or data, etc.)

Medical Background

What, if any, is your religious background? (Both family and your present religious status)

```

```

Any type of history of alcohol or drug abuse?

```

```

Any type of history of Mental Illness? If yes, please explain:

```

```

Any type of history of serious trauma? (Ex: Near Death, rape, etc.)

```

```

List all medications and prescription items used in the past three years. Include all prescriptions drugs, over-the-counter drugs, prescription eyeglasses, contact lenses, etc. Please make a separate list for each occupant.

```

```

Have anyone's prescriptions changed recently?

```

```

Any other family history that you can think of is important?

```

```

When did the current disturbances begin, and what happened at first?

What did you think of these disturbances?

Have you looked for ordinary, normal explanations? What makes you think it's paranormal?

When did the most recent incident occur, and what happened?

Have the disturbances been increasing in frequency and/or severity since they first began?

Are events more frequent at certain times of the day, days of weeks, or particular months? If so, what times?

Is there a pattern of any kind to these disturbances that you've noticed (i.e., when the events occurred, what sorts of objects were affected, what locations were involved, who was around at the time, etc.)?

Is activity more frequent in certain places (for example, in certain rooms of the house) than in others? If so, where?

Do the occurrences happen more frequently in the presence or vicinity of certain persons than they do with others? If so, state which people. Also, do the events take place when they are not in the area?

Have there been any witnesses from outside the household? What did they experience, as far as you know?

Has anyone ever seen an object start to move when no one was near it? If so, describe all such occurrences.

If there have been unexplained movements of objects, was there anything strange about the manner in which the objects moved or stopped? (e.g., objects that move around corners, or hit with unusually great force, etc.)

Have you or anyone in the residence ever used or experimented with Ouija Boards, séances, etc.?

Have you or anyone in the residence ever used or experimented with the Occult (Witchcraft, Magick, Quabalah) or used any type of Occult practices for personal gain? (e.g., money, love, revenge, etc.) If so, please explain:

How would you like to be helped?

Have any of the occupants encountered any of the following? (Explain all that apply.)

Voices	
Smells/Odors	
Shadows	
Orbs	
Smoky Forms	
Strong Random Thoughts	
Strong Feelings /Emotions	
Cold Spots	
Hot Spots	
Recent Death of Loved One	
Recent Anniversary of Loved One's Death, Birthday, Anniversary, etc.	
Sounds (Walking, running, knocking, etc.)	
Door(s) Opening/Closing	
Mood Changes, especially in one room	
Conversations with Spirits	
Disappearing Objects	
Objects Moving	
Puberty of Family Member or Emotional Stress of Adolescents in area	
Renovations to Location	
Electrical Disturbances (frequent light bulb burnouts, etc)	
Problems with Appliances (TV, Radio, Stereo, Computers, Clocks, Microwave, etc.)	
Headaches or dizziness	
Feeling of being touched	
Physical harm (scratches, cuts, bites, etc.)	

RESEARCH

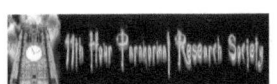

INVESTIGATION REPORT

Client/Location:		Investigation Date:	
Address:			
Client Email:		Client Phone:	

Team Leader:		Report Date:	
Start Time:		End Time:	

Investigators

List all investigators present at this investigation. List specific positions assigned to each investigator if applicable (ie, lead, tech support, client liaison, medium, etc.)

Name	Position for This Investigation	Equipment Used

Site Observations

Describe your observations of the investigation site as collected by all investigators detailing the condition of the property and environment. Please be as descriptive as possible and note any changes in the environment as the investigation progresses.

Type of Site:	☐ residential ☐ commercial property Description:	
Site Conditions:		
Client/Contact:		
Weather Conditions:		
Other Observations:		

Debunk Report

List any potential or proven natural explanations for reported claims of activity collected by all investigators.

Time	Reported Claim	Investigator	Explanation of Cause

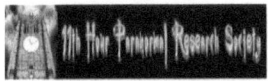

Page 1 of 4

- 121 -

Investigation Report (continued)

Time	Investigator	Evidence or Observation
Investigation Timeline Log		
List any evidence gathered, observations and experiences during the investigation as collected by all investigators.		

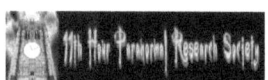

Investigation Report (continued)

Evidence Review

List any potential evidence gathered during evidence review as collected by all investigators. Note the type of evidence and describe the surrounding circumstances of the occurrence:

Time	Type of Evidence	Description
	☐ video ☐ audio ☐ photo ☐ other data	
	☐ video ☐ audio ☐ photo ☐ other data	
	☐ video ☐ audio ☐ photo ☐ other data	
	☐ video ☐ audio ☐ photo ☐ other data	
	☐ video ☐ audio ☐ photo ☐ other data	
	☐ video ☐ audio ☐ photo ☐ other data	
	☐ video ☐ audio ☐ photo ☐ other data	
	☐ video ☐ audio ☐ photo ☐ other data	
	☐ video ☐ audio ☐ photo ☐ other data	
	☐ video ☐ audio ☐ photo ☐ other data	
	☐ video ☐ audio ☐ photo ☐ other data	
	☐ video ☐ audio ☐ photo ☐ other data	
	☐ video ☐ audio ☐ photo ☐ other data	
	☐ video ☐ audio ☐ photo ☐ other data	
	☐ video ☐ audio ☐ photo ☐ other data	
	☐ video ☐ audio ☐ photo ☐ other data	
	☐ video ☐ audio ☐ photo ☐ other data	
	☐ video ☐ audio ☐ photo ☐ other data	
	☐ video ☐ audio ☐ photo ☐ other data	
	☐ video ☐ audio ☐ photo ☐ other data	
	☐ video ☐ audio ☐ photo ☐ other data	
	☐ video ☐ audio ☐ photo ☐ other data	
	☐ video ☐ audio ☐ photo ☐ other data	
	☐ video ☐ audio ☐ photo ☐ other data	

Noteworthy Evidence

Describe any noteworthy evidence, experiences, observations or debunked claims gathered documented above that may be pertinent to the outcome or resolution of this investigation. Describe any potential natural causes of your findings and note any supporting material.

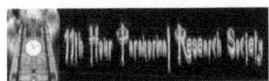

Investigation Report (continued)

Summary & Suggestions
Please summarize your thoughts on this investigation and note your suggestions for follow-up or resolution of this case.

Suggest Follow-Up Investigation? ☐ Yes ☐ No

Recommended Next Steps:

INVESTIGATION REPORT

Client/Location:		Investigation Date:	

Investigator Name:		Report Date:	
Start Time:		End Time:	

Site Observations

Describe your observations of the investigation site detailing the condition of the property and environment. Please be as descriptive as possible and note any changes in the environment as the investigation progresses.

Type of Site:	☐ residential ☐ commercial property	Description:
Site Conditions:		
Client/Contact:		
Weather Conditions:		
Other Observations:		

Equipment Used

List equipment you used during the investigation including the model. Detail the settings and any accessories attached.

Type / Model	Settings and Accessories Used

Debunk Report

List any potential or proven natural explanations for reported claims of activity

Time	Reported Claim	Explanation of Cause

Investigation Timeline Log

List any evidence gathered, observations and experiences during the investigation. Please be as descriptive as possible.

Time	Evidence or Observation

Investigation Timeline (continued)

Time	Evidence or Observation

Evidence Review

List any potential evidence gathered during evidence review. Note the type of evidence and describe the surrounding circumstances of the occurrence

Time	Type of Evidence	Description
	☐ video ☐ audio ☐ photo ☐ other data	
	☐ video ☐ audio ☐ photo ☐ other data	
	☐ video ☐ audio ☐ photo ☐ other data	
	☐ video ☐ audio ☐ photo ☐ other data	
	☐ video ☐ audio ☐ photo ☐ other data	
	☐ video ☐ audio ☐ photo ☐ other data	
	☐ video ☐ audio ☐ photo ☐ other data	
	☐ video ☐ audio ☐ photo ☐ other data	
	☐ video ☐ audio ☐ photo ☐ other data	
	☐ video ☐ audio ☐ photo ☐ other data	
	☐ video ☐ audio ☐ photo ☐ other data	
	☐ video ☐ audio ☐ photo ☐ other data	
	☐ video ☐ audio ☐ photo ☐ other data	

Noteworthy Evidence

Describe any noteworthy evidence, experiences, observations or debunked claims gathered documented above that may be pertinent to the outcome or resolution of this investigation. Describe any potential natural causes of your findings and note any supporting material.

 11th Hour Paranormal Research Society

Summary & Suggestions
Please summarize your thoughts on this investigation and note your suggestions for follow-up or resolution of this case.

www.ingramcontent.com/pod-product-compliance
Lightning Source LLC
Chambersburg PA
CBHW051412280526
45785CB00003B/1037